THE TEACHING OF HISTORY

The Teaching of History

DENNIS GUNNING

CROOM HELM
London & Canberra

© 1978 Dennis Gunning
Croom Helm Ltd, Provident House, Burrell Row,
Beckenham, Kent BR3 1AT
Croom Helm Australia Pty Ltd, 28 Kembla Street,
Fyshwick, ACT 2609, Australia
Reprinted 1979, 1980 and 1984

British Library Cataloguing in Publication Data

Gunning, Dennis
　　The teaching of history.
　　1. History – Study and teaching (Secondary) –
　　Great Britain
　　I. Title
　　907'.12'41　　D16.4G7

　　ISBN 0-85664-762-4

Pictures courtesy of: National Maritime Museum, page 43; Imperial War Museum, pages 44 and 45; Victoria and Albert Museum, page 46; Hulton Picture Library, page 77; John Krish, page 78; Cambridge University Press, Anna Mieke and Barry Eyden, pages 91 and 109; National Museum of Wales, page 108; Bibliotheque Nationale, Paris, page 92. The picture on page 48 is the property of the author.

Printed and bound in Great Britain by
Biddles Ltd, Guildford and King's Lynn

CONTENTS

ACKNOWLEDGEMENTS

I would like to thank here the authorities of Trent Polytechnic, Nottingham, who gave me the secondment time to work up the teaching materials which form the core of this book, and also the local teachers, particularly Mr S. Ryan and Mr D.J. Mahoney of Manvers School, Nottingham, who have been so helpful to me.

The support and encouragement of my wife, Stella, have been indispensable.

D.G.

INTRODUCTION

'I know I'm supposed to keep the class active, not just listening to me, but I soon run out of ideas of how to do that.'

'I try discussion with 3T, but they just can't sustain it. Gary and Tony talk a bit and two or three others, then it just fades out.'

'I use task sheets. I know I should grade them according to the ability of the different kids, but how do you do that in history? It's not like Maths!'

'I've inherited two textbooks for the whole class. One is a lot too hard, the other is childish.'

'Look, I've got examination classes. So all this new fancy method stuff is irrelevant. They have to learn the facts!'

This book is designed to help teachers of history to solve problems of classroom teaching, like those described or hinted at in the five quotations above.[1] It will try to set out a clear set of principles, illustrated by detailed examples and backed up by 'exercises' in which the reader can try to apply the principles, to see how far they work, or make sense.

Before we can come to the principles on which we are going to work, we ought to understand something about the background of recent thinking about the question of the status of history as a subject, and the related question of how to learn and teach it.

Some Current Theories about History Teaching

In recent years there have been three main influences: Piaget, Bruner and Bloom. Piaget has been responsible for a greatly increased awareness of the importance of concepts in the learning or teaching of anything, including historical material. Some people have even been led to the extreme (but unnecessary) conclusion that since history is full of abstract concepts, it is not suitable as a subject at all for students under sixteen. Even if one does not go as far as that, the influence of Piagetian studies has certainly been in the direction of caution. As we shall see later in this section, a proposition like 'the peasants attacked the aristocrats' might once have been seen as a very straightforward piece of 'information' to be learned. We are more likely now to see it as a sentence containing two concepts, 'peasant' and 'aristocrat', which are both likely to be less than fully understood by many students in almost *any* age-ability grouping.

The influence of Jerome Bruner is many-sided and complex, but its two important aspects are: first, hostility to the idea of subjects as bodies of information to be passed on from teacher to learner, an insistence on the importance of learning concepts, procedures and skills and, more specifically, the idea that the main concern of a learner should be to learn what Bruner calls 'the structures of subjects', i.e the *characteristic* concepts, skills and mode of enquiry of a given subject. This, in turn, leads on to the idea that the central goal of a learner who is 'doing' history is to learn the characteristic procedures of a professional historian and to master the central concepts of the historical discipline, like 'evidence', 'source' and the notion of the tentative, provisional nature of historical judgements. Second, an insistence that the learning of these concepts and procedures can and should start very early in a child's school life. This is embodied in the famous idea of the 'spiral curriculum' which might be crudely illustrated by this example: a young child might have the following understanding about kings: 'They wear crowns and sit on a throne.' We might get that child to add to this idea the notion that kings give orders. Months later, he might be helped to refine this idea even further to 'kings give orders, but not crazy orders.' Later still, he can add the idea that the king has people to help him work out what orders to give and so on. Eventually we hope for a full-blown understanding of the idea of kingship on the pupil's part, but Bruner's great point is that we do not wait around for that full understanding to emerge at age twelve or fourteen, or whatever, and act disappointed when it fails to appear; but to work at producing the understanding, in a planned, conscious way, by expanding the growing understanding in appropriate ways at age six, nine, ten and so on.

The third major influence is the work of Bloom and his associates, from whom we get the powerful idea of the possibility of drawing up a list, or even a hierarchy, of cognitive skills. There has been much controversy about whether Bloom's particular list of skills is the most helpful and whether or not it truly constitutes a hierarchy. However that may be, the idea of 'skills' is of immense importance to teachers of history. Teachers for many years agreed that, as well as conveying information, they were getting their students to develop certain skills. What these skills were was vaguely and variously expressed: 'to think for themselves', 'to think clearly', 'organise written work', 'write essays', 'express themselves clearly' and so on. Bloom and others

have indicated that we can set ourselves vastly more precise targets
in this area than 'think clearly' or 'write essays'. No teacher's armoury
is now complete without some fairly precise answer to the question:
'What am I going to make them better at doing?'

These three major influences have combined with other influences,
notably from the field of language studies, to produce a marked
development in creative thinking about history and connected fields
of study. Quite a lot of confused thinking has also, inevitably, gone on.
Many other issues have been raised, such as the question of whether
history should be taught separately or as a part of an integrated
humanities system, issues with which this book will not be directly
concerned.

It is, however, still rather difficult, despite some fifteen years of
research and development in this field, to work out a simple answer
to problems like the five posed on the first page of this section.

The approach we will use is a fairly simple one, based on two ideas.
First, the primacy of the importance of grasping concepts in understanding historical material. No complicated model of a 'concept
structure of the subject', in the Bruner style, will be offered. Secondly,
the vital importance of students' learning of intellectual skills. The idea
of learning a set of skills peculiar to historians will not be put forward,
mainly because it is arguably too restricting an idea. Also, the
question, 'Why should all pupils learn the skills of professional
academics?' does not yet seem to me to have been satisfactorily
answered.

For beginners, the best course would probably be to accept these
two premises for the moment: the primacy of concept-learning and
the vital importance of skill-learning. Use this book to acquire some
skill in the arts of setting tasks involving development of concepts and
skills and then read the books in the 'further reading' book list. If you
decide after your reading that, say, the idea of 'the skills of the
historian' is one you agree with, then you can easily adapt what you
have learned to that particular philosophical slant.

However, this book's playing down of the emphasis on the specific
concepts and special skills 'of the subject' takes us into opposition to
some of the most distinguished recent thinkers in the field, so it needs a
little expansion.

Briefly, our position is this. There is an academic discipline called
'History'. There is also a school subject called 'History'. There is no
self-evident reason why they have to be the same. If we are teaching
fourteen-year-olds, we should subject everything we want to teach

them, whether a fact, a concept or a skill, to this question: 'Of what use, or potential use, is this knowledge to them?' We should not ask, 'Is this piece of knowledge, or this skill, part of the equipment of an academic historian?' because the vast majority of our pupils will never be academic historians.

Most of the time, of course, there is a lot of overlap, since knowledge and skills useful to historians are very often useful also to parents, citizens and other people and therefore potentially of use to our students. But not always. The 'discipline of history' idea can lead, for instance, to students being given historical documents to interpret in the original crabbed, illegible script in which they were written, on the grounds that construing crabbed, illegible script is a thing historians do. So it is, but young students have a great many more important things to be learning, and any theory that leads to them spending time on palaeography needs a lot of defending.

Concepts: A Definition

Before we can put flesh on these bones and describe our guiding principles in more detail, we must say what we mean by a 'concept'. Very many different definitions of 'concept' have been offered by psychologists and philosophers, and what we need is a serviceable working definition. It could go like this:

(1)   Napoleon I is not a concept, because there was only one of him. 'Emperor', however, is a concept. In other words: *Concepts are ideas, usually expressed in words, to describe classes or groups of things, people, feelings, actions or ideas having something in common, e.g. emperors, artillery, princes, envy, retreat or liberalism.*

(2)   Some concepts we could illustrate, quite literally, by drawing or showing somebody a picture of the thing in question. 'Sword', for instance, is a concept because it describes a class of things. A picture of a sword, or a model, would be the quickest way to make clear to someone what it is that swords as a class have in common, which marks them off from guns, spears or penknives. *'Concepts' can be ideas describing concrete actual objects.*

(3)   We would have a hard time, though, showing somebody an object to represent the concept 'economics', and this other class of concept, the abstract type, is very thick on the ground in history. *Many concepts are abstract, for instance 'economics'.*

(4)   Finally, we should note this: most of our examples, so far, like 'Napoleon' and 'economics', have all been nouns. But a concept

like 'rebellion' could well appear in the form of a verb, to rebel, or an adjective, rebellious. *A concept idea is not always presented in words which are nouns.*

If you put together the four italicised sentences, you should have a serviceable definition of 'concept'. If I were to ask you, now, to pick out the concepts in a piece of prose, I should say, strictly speaking, 'Pick out the words embodying concepts.' As a shorthand, though, from now on we will use phrases like 'try to find the main concepts here', not the more accurate, longer formula.

The Primacy of Concepts

Let us take a case: suppose you had to teach the French Revolution to a class of fourteen-year-olds. Leave aside for the moment questions about whether the French Revolution is a worthwhile topic, where it would fit in a whole curriculum and so on. As we start to plan how to teach the topic, one thing should emerge straight away: if students are going to understand about the French Revolution, they will need to understand a fairly large number of quite abstract concepts, for instance 'revolution', 'discontent', 'peasant', 'monarchy', 'aristocrat', 'middle class' and so on.

Now, many in the class will have an imperfect, or actually wrong, understanding of these concepts. So if we start in to teach as if everybody did understand, then all we are heading for is disappointment. This is why attempts to treat history as if it were a body of information to be conveyed, of 'facts to be got across', are doomed. Most of the time, in the case of most topics, with most students, the information is in large part not clearly understood and often actually meaningless to the students. When we say, 'The peasants were discontented and attacked the aristocrats', it is difficult to convey what that apparently simple idea might sound like to a student of fourteen. It is not as if the *words* 'peasant' and 'aristocrat' were unknown to them, not as if we were saying 'The slurge were discontented and attacked the Klunz'. If the case were like that, then students might at least ask us what the strange words meant. Some actual students very much older than fourteen thought that 'peasant' meant 'a foolish person, improvident, feckless'. Some of them also thought that an aristocrat was 'a member of the royal family'. Now try reading 'The peasants were discontented and attacked the aristocrats' in the light of those two 'understandings'.

We cannot avoid the use of abstractions, even if we try. We might say 'king' instead of 'monarchy', 'farmer' for 'peasant', but there are limits to such a process. Even if we could both simplify our vocabulary and yet not sound as if we were addressing eight-year-olds, there is still the matter of the language the class will meet in textbooks and reference books. We really do not want to sidestep the problem of concepts such as 'peasant' anyway, because they are very useful ones to understand. They are useful for understanding many historical matters besides the French Revolution and perhaps even more to the point, understanding of them can transfer to a huge number of other situations and contexts of a social, economic or political nature.

You can choose one of two intellectual tracks at this point, and which one you take is a matter of individual choice. You could say, 'My aim as a history teacher is to promote understanding of history. My main aim in doing the French Revolution with this class is that they shall understand and remember about the French Revolution. To achieve that end, a vital subsidiary aim I must have is to ensure that they extend their understanding of the following terms: "revolution", "discontent", "peasant", etc.' Or you could say: 'My aim as a history teacher is for students to develop their understanding of concepts like "revolution", "discontent", "peasant", etc. I choose the French Revolution as my instrument in this task because it illustrates the ideas in a colourful, dramatic and interesting way. If, in say five years' time, the students don't recall too much about the details of the French Revolution, I will not mind, so long as their grasp of the concepts is sound.'

Which of these lines you take depends on your general attitude to history teaching and to a good many things outside the scope of this book. The important things are these: whichever line you take, the question of fostering pupils' understanding of concepts should now take a central place in your planning of your teaching. By 'concepts' you mean not just broad general categories like 'communication' or 'power', and not just concepts to do with history as a subject, like 'evidence', but large numbers of concepts specific to the understanding of specific topics – in our present case 'revolution', 'peasant', 'aristocrat', etc.

The Necessity of Teaching Skills

If we stay with the French Revolution example, we can get a line on our second guiding principle, to do with intellectual skills. Suppose in the course of the topic we asked the class, 'What if the Prussians had won the battle of Valmy in 1792, what would have happened?'

Compare these two responses.

> Student A: 'Prussians would have got to Paris and Revolution
> would have to be over.'
> Student B: 'The Prussians might get to Paris, but the peasants would
> fight still for land in guerrilla war.'

Both students have had to use what Bloom calls the skill of *extrapolation*. They have had to think about the nature of revolution. Student B has arguably thought to more purpose and knows better than A that a revolution is not the kind of thing you turn on and off like a tap, just because somebody loses a battle. The main point, though, is that the use of the skill has caused the students to consider the concept and thereby both to reveal their understanding of it to the teacher and to extend their understanding of it, however marginally.

Being able to extrapolate well, i.e. using all the available evidence intelligently, sounds like a very useful thing to be able to do in any circumstances. It is not *particularly* a thing that historians do, though some might do it sometimes. If we approach the question of skills only by way of the question, 'What are the skills of the historian?' we get too narrow an answer. It is better to ask: 'What skills can a student learn which will help in concept development, which are also worthwhile for their own sake?' We might now try to summarise our position:

(a)   From Bruner and Piaget we take the idea of the central importances of concept development.

(b)   From Bloom we take the idea of the possibility of isolating and developing specific, named intellectual skills.

(c)   We play down the idea of 'the key concepts of the subject' and offer instead the idea of 'the large number of specific social, political, economic concepts involved in the understanding of any historical topic'.

(d)   We also play down the idea of 'the skills of the historian' in favour of concentration on a wider range of skills (though, as will emerge, the two categories obviously overlap a lot).

Notes

1.   We assume throughout the book that the teacher has a history class and is

not working in any kind of integrated humanities scheme. This is done only for convenience. The question of the merits of subject-based or 'integrated' work is beyond the scope of this book.

2.   The actual scheme of 'skills' used is not that of Bloom, though obviously derived from it. It is a pretty crude simplification of Bloom's very sophisticated work and the only virtue claimed for it is serviceability.

3.   The term 'students' throughout refers to any pupils between 11 and 18 years of age.

4.   Exercises: Some people might find it pretty patronising to be asked to do 'exercises' and even, sometimes, referred to an 'answers' section to check out their responses to the exercises. This book is partly aimed at beginners, though, and beginners need to apply principles by means of 'exercises' in some shape or form, whatever we call them. Once having set exercises, it seemed only right, where possible, to answer the inevitable question: 'What would you do?' hence the 'comments and answers' sections.

1 CONCEPTS

1. Deciding Which Concepts to Teach

If we decide that trying to get students to understand a wide range of concepts is going to be one of our fundamental aims, we then have to decide which specific concepts will be taught. There are three ways in which concepts may crop up:

(1)   If, as often happens, somebody prescribes for us the historical topics which we are to cover and even the books we are to use, we must be able to work out in advance which main concepts are inevitably going to be encountered by pupils in their reading or in any simple exposition we might give ourselves, or in any work they might do on that topic.

(2)   Given a topic to cover, we need to be able to designate a few concepts which would not necessarily arise in working on the topic, but which we could conveniently and appropriately introduce ourselves, if we chose.

(3)   If we were given a free hand to plan the work of a class in history, we ought to be able to construct a syllabus partly in terms of those important concepts which we want students to learn.

Let us take the problems one by one. First − if we were given a prescribed topic to cover, there is one crude but effective way to proceed. Write a very short, very plain account of the topic in about thirty to fifty words. Then go through your account underlining terms denoting concepts which you think could be imperfectly understood by any student in the class you are preparing to teach − erring on the side of pessimism at this point.

Supposing that the English Civil War was our topic and we had a class of thirteen-year-olds, the end result of our preliminary exercise might look like this: 'In 1642, *civil war* broke out between the King and *Parliament*. Many battles were fought, though at first they were not *decisive*. The main weapons used were *pikes* and *muskets*. In the end, Parliament *won*.' If a student had no idea, or a very wrong idea, about the meaning of the underlined words, he would pretty clearly be unable to understand the passage, and so, after a short time, would not be able even to recall the gist of it and would, therefore, be poorly placed for learning, understanding and recalling things about the Civil War.

Next, we can usefully break the problem into three parts. Of all the terms emphasised, the easiest to explain are 'pike' and 'musket', because these terms have what we call concrete referents, i.e. you could in principle show a person a pike and say 'This is a pike.' In practice, you could draw a picture, show a picture, show a model, etc.

The other terms are all *abstractions*. Some of them are of obvious difficulty, e.g. Parliament, Civil War. These are the kind of semi-technical terms characteristic of writing or speech about history which are fairly easy to spot with a little practice.

That leaves two terms, 'decisive' and 'won'. These words are not easy to spot as difficult abstractions which might cause pupils trouble. They are not particularly 'history' words and could well occur in almost any context, especially 'won'. And, most tricky of all, as in the case of 'won', they often don't even sound difficult. However, a pupil's ready acceptance and apparent understanding of an apparently simple term like 'won' could conceal any or all of the following misunderstandings of the idea of 'winning'; in this instance:

(1)   'All the King's army was killed.'
(2)   'The King was killed.'
(3)   'All the King's followers changed their minds and supported Parliament.'

We might call words like 'won' and 'decisive' 'weasel words'. A few further examples are given below in italics:

(1)   The Bolsheviks gained *control* of Russia.
(2)   The Church *controlled* education.
(3)   *Unrest* spread through the country.
(4)   There was *discontent* with the republic.
(5)   Murad Agha established his *rule* over the oasis.
(6)   The UN General Assembly *attacked* the National Assembly as undemocratic.

'Weasel words' have two important characteristics. They do not always leap to the eye as difficult, especially if there are other, more obviously hard words, near them (for example, notice how, in the example above, if we are seeking possible sources of difficulty we tend to notice terms like Bolshevik, Church, republic, oasis, General

Assembly, National Assembly, undemocratic). Second, when we think about it, our *own* understanding of them is often a bit vague. We have been content, sometimes, in our reading and thinking, to slur over them, content with a hazy, partial understanding; for example, how clear a picture is brought to your mind by the sentence 'The Church controlled education'?

The second problem, that of adding on concepts which do not unavoidably have to be dealt with, but which you positively want to deal with, may not come up at all. It may be that you have found so many concepts to deal with which are unavoidable that you don't want to add to the list. However, if we go back to our original English Civil War case, you might think you could deal with 'pike' and 'Parliament' and the rest of them, and still have time for more.

It is important to decide exactly which concepts you want to add. It is easy to say at this stage:

> This stuff about pikes and Parliaments is just the surface of things
> – I want students to see that this Civil War in England was a tragic
> event, that families were divided among themselves; I want them to
> get the feel of what this war meant for British history – that is the
> concept I want to add.

Actually, this statement contains a *judgement* (that the Civil War was tragic), a *fact* (that families were split) and an idea of doubtful meaning ('the feel of what this war meant'). A cooler way of thinking might produce a clearer outcome.

The first move is to think out what area or aspect we want our 'extra' concept to be in. The imaginary teacher quoted above is plainly interested in the fact that the issues of the war were deeply felt, so deeply as to divide families. So he might try writing a short, plain sentence or so on that theme: 'Many people chose sides in this war from strong *convictions*. So sometimes, even if a father chose one side, his son would choose the other. The *issues* went on *dividing people* long after the war itself was over.' So our extra commitment clarifies itself; we have three additional concepts that we want students to grasp: 'convictions', 'issues' and 'dividing people'. Try this technique now to work out what additional concepts you yourself might want to bring in to this Civil War topic.

Our next case presents a different sort of problem – someone has said to you, 'Cover some twentieth-century history with this class of fourteen-year-olds this year – write your own syllabus, you have a free hand.' Let us leave aside for now the constraints imposed by time available, books available and so on and think about this question: would a syllabus made up with concept development clearly in mind look any different from a conventionally planned syllabus?

We have to make a small apparent digression here. Our main problem as history teachers is not going to be with explaining pikes and Zeppelins, but with abstractions. In the first place, it is only a shorthand to speak of people 'knowing' abstractions, or 'learning' them. The following passages all attempted to define the English seventeenth-century Parliament:

(1)   'Parliament was the King's friends, they went about with him.'
(2)   'People used to choose men to speak for them about what they wanted doing. The chosen men were called Parliament.'
(3)   'Parliament was mostly rich men, chosen by other fairly rich men, to makes laws, and run the country.'
(4)   'Parliament was a constantly shifting set of interest groups, in a constantly shifting relationship with the Crown.'

Writer (4), we might guess, has a very firm grasp of the concept of Parliament. But plainly we cannot say that (3) and (2) have *no* understanding of the concept. Even (1) understands that Parliament was a body of people in some sort of relationship to the King, so we cannot even say that (1) has no understanding of the concept. We talk, therefore, of people having *an* understanding of a concept, and of *improving* their understanding. If we have to teach the seventeenth century to a given class, we ask not 'Do they understand what "Parliament" means?' but 'What understanding of the concept of Parliament do they have?'

A second characteristic really follows from the first: a once-for-all explanation of an abstract concept is not sufficient. People extend and improve their understanding of concepts by using them, in speech and writing, in a great variety of ways. We might want to speak of 'teaching' the concept of Parliament, because it is cumbersome to always say, 'I am procuring an extension of the understanding of . . .' That is quite acceptable so long as we remember that 'teaching a concept' extends over months rather than minutes and involves pupils engaging in all manner of activities, using the concept, not simply being told what it means, however carefully. We shall return soon to this question of how to 'teach concepts' in the chapter on

'Intellectual Skills'.

For the moment, however, the main point is that if concepts are not best dealt with by a once-for-all attack, this gives us an important guiding idea for building a syllabus for a year. We could say that we will plan for a given set of concepts to be attacked, using different illustrative historical material of course, more than once in the course of the year.

This could be an insanely complicated method, if we try to plan for work on, say, the concept of 'conscription' to occur in late October, early March, third week of June and so on. So we will plan simply to divide the year into two halves and plan to have the same main concepts dealt with in the second half as in the first, using a different set of illustrative material.

When it comes to designating the actual concepts to be dealt with, the teacher is ultimately alone with his own idea of what is important. The idea of 'over-arching' concepts, ideas at a very high level of generality, like 'conflict' or 'communication', as guiding principles really does not give a lot of help when we are required to particularise a syllabus on the twentieth century. We might proceed, as we did before, by making 'brief statements' to ourselves as it were, in answer to the question: 'What are the three or four most important circumstances, events or ideas that an educated person ought to know of, and understand, as a result of learning about twentieth-century history?'

For convenience, we could divide the area into three parts, on traditional lines, political, economic and social. Here is the kind of result we might get, by way of illustration.

Political: Main ideas (1) socialism and nationalism in their various forms. How socialism and nationalism seem to run together in Third World 'liberation movements' after 1945. (2) War. Many wars, on a great scale, great effects. World War I, World War II, Vietnam.

Economic: (3) Prosperity and (4) the argument over state intervention in the economy.

Social: (5) Idea of many rapid changes of attitude to women, black people, children, sex, the arts, etc.

If we now try to write short statements about each of our five main ideas, emphasising the abstractions, including 'weasel words', we will get a set of concept lists, concepts which are particular to our concerns, in this particular area of history.

One example might be helpful:

> '*Socialism*' is an *economic* idea and a *political* idea. On economics socialists generally agree that *wealth* ought not to be *distributed* as it is under *capitalist* arrangements, but should be *owned* and *controlled* by the *working class* or *proletariat* or *peasants*. On politics, some believe in *revolution* followed by *dictatorship*, at least for a time, others in *democratic procedures*.

This statement is 59 words long, which is forgiveable in a statement on a very complex idea, but try to make none of your 'statements' any longer than that. *Twentieth-century war*, for instance, we might do as briefly as this:

> First we had *mass conscript* armies, fighting huge *mechanised* wars, with a huge *industrial base*. *Total* war, for example bombing of *civilians*. After 1945, more *guerrilla* wars, *terrorism* and great use of *publicity* and *propaganda*. [34 words]

We have now five general areas, five 'brief statements' and five lists of fairly specific concepts. Now we have to choose what material to use to illustrate them and make a vehicle for developing understanding of them, not once but twice over, in the two halves of the year.

We have to weigh up several factors:

(a)   Which material will give the most clear and convenient basis for understanding the given concepts? For instance, the National Socialist movement seems a good example of the twentieth-century phenomenon of the 'running together' of the themes of nationalism and socialism; but is it too confusing an example, since the 'socialism' was so nominal? Would African nationalism in the 1960s be better?

(b)   Which material are the students likely to find most stimulating and interesting?

(c)   Suppose we could deal with all the concepts quite well using only the history of western Europe and the USA. Should we nevertheless try to use African, Asian, Latin American material on general grounds?

(d)   Should we try to keep to chronological order, or use themes?

Will the students be confused by a non-chronological approach?

(e) With our main idea number 5, change of attitudes in the course of the twentieth century, we probably cannot successfully deal in the time with attitudes to women, black people, children, sex and the arts — if we have to choose just two, which two will it be?

All these questions call for you to make evaluations of a personal kind, so for the next stage, we will simply assume that the following choices were made.

First Half-Year

Broadly chronological approach
World War I ('war' group of concepts)
Russian Revolution and Stalin ('socialism' concepts)
America and the Great Depression ('socialism' concepts, 'prosperity' and 'state intervention' concepts)
The Irish Rebellion 1916-21 ('nationalism' group of concepts)
The women's movement ('changes in attitude' concepts)

Second Half-Year

'Thematic' approach
World War II, the Arab-Israeli dispute and Vietnam ('war' group of concepts)
Chinese Revolution and China since 1949   ('socialism' and the
Labour movement, Britain since 1945   economic concepts)
African nationalism, Indian nationalism ('nationalism' and 'socialism')
Black people in USA since 1945 ('attitude changes' group of concepts)

We now have an outline syllabus. Apart from the rather careful matching up of the two halves of the year, it is not a particularly unconventional one except in one respect, that it leaves quite large gaps. For instance, there is nothing on the rise of Hitler or the origins of World War II.

At this point you could do one of three things:

(1) You could recognise that your initial working-out of the five main areas of concern was faulty, and that it is essential to add in say, the rise of Hitler. Bear in mind that we have already about twelve major areas to do. Postulating a 36-week year, that gives about three weeks per area. Some of the areas, like America and the Depression,

for instance, seem to contain a large number of difficult and important ideas, which we will be hard pressed to deal with adequately in three weeks.

(2)   You could put in the rise of Hitler, take something else out and reorder the plan.

(3)   You could decide that one mark of a syllabus that tries to make careful provision for concept learning and concept strengthening is that it cannot be over-stuffed with content. Selection, therefore, has to be very ruthless, quite simply because worthwhile, structured learning takes a lot longer than just covering historical ground. So Hitler's rise is best left out.

We now know how to work out a concept list to form the basis of our planning for teaching in either of two situations; from scratch, or from the 'givens' of a syllabus written by somebody else.

There is one more thing we can do to provide ourselves with a fairly complete answer to the question, 'What concepts are we going to be dealing with?' Giving an explanation of an abstraction often involves using other abstractions. In a moment we shall deal, under the heading 'Giving Explanations of Concepts', with ways of reducing this difficulty, but there is no complete way round it. You might, for example, find that you just cannot sensibly explain 'revolution' without using the term 'government'.

So we should take our concept list and as our last preliminary planning move, rough out brief explanations of all the concepts. If explaining an abstraction throws up other abstractions, then add those abstractions to the list and try explaining *them*. Keep up the process until you are confident that there is no concept left that you cannot explain in concrete terms, or at least in terms you are quite confident your student will understand.

Exercise

Try explaining complex abstractions like 'revolution', 'capitalism', 'nationalism', or a similar idea of your own choosing, noting the abstract concepts you have to use in explaining the original concept. Then try explaining *those* concepts in their turn until your get down to ideas you can explain without using abstract language.

2. Giving Explanations of Concepts

The safest rule is to become as skilled as you can in explaining abstract concepts by reference to the concrete, avoiding reference to other abstractions as far as possible. The following illustrates the point: the first 'explanation' in each case involves a tangle of further abstract concepts, perhaps more difficult than the idea being 'explained'.

(1)   Tactics

(a)   'Tactics are the means employed by a commander to defeat the enemy in a given situation.'

(b)

  'Look at this diagram. We would say that General C's *tactics* were to send some of his men to attack the enemy (**B**) from the front, and others to attack from the side.'

(c)   'Suppose you had a soccer team planning their next match, deciding things like how many men to have in defence, what to do at corners and free kicks and so on. We could say that they were planning their *tactics*.'

(2)   Unrest

(a)   'Unrest is manifestation of discontent — it can be social, or political, or both.'

(b)   'People saying the government is no good, people attacking the police, or not paying taxes, people being very unhappy about something going on in the country, that's *unrest*.'

(c)   'Suppose they brought in a new school rule that everyone had to wear ties. Suppose a lot of kids wouldn't and people wrote 'down with the tie rule' on walls, some people even broke windows and things because they were so upset by the rule. Then we'd say there was *unrest* in the school.'

(3)   Radical (nineteenth century)

(a)   'Radicalism involved making more fundamental attacks on institutions and putting forward more far-reaching plans for reform.'

(b)   'Suppose a man had the idea that, say, Wales ought to have its own Parliament and make some of its own laws and suppose a second man said Wales ought to be entirely separate from Britain and make all its own laws. We would say that the second man was taking a more radical line.'

(c)   'Suppose the bus fares went up a lot. Suppose some of you said, "Let's write to the council and complain the fares are too high" and suppose others said "No, let's write and say that school students should travel free on the buses anyway" — we could say the second lot were being *radicals*.'

Notice how in 1 (b), 1 (c), 2 (b), 2 (c), 3 (b) and 3 (c) the explanation does not start with the words in question. The word occurs near the end, or actually *at* the end of the explanation. This is a good piece of technique to copy. Research indicates that it is often the more effective method to 'build up' to the newly-learned word in this way.

Now try your hand at explaining the following terms: peasant, revolution, dictator, emigrants, investment.

In the above examples, we have imagined the explainer speaking as if the concept in question was quite new to his audience. Sometimes this is how we have to do it if the pupil has no grasp at all of the new concept, or is completely mistaken (for example, if he thought that 'radicals' meant 'Frenchmen'). Very often, though, the pupils have *an* understanding, but not an adequate one.

Let us take the 'Parliament' examples of imperfect understanding on page 22. The ideal to aim for is to accept and use whatever understanding the pupil already has. So in the case of student 1, we would not say 'No, no, it's nothing to do with the King, it's like this . . .', but rather on these lines:

Suppose there was something we wanted to tell the King, like there's a great many robbers round here causing trouble — we wouldn't all go to London to tell him, we would choose one of us to go, perhaps the best talker. The one chosen would go to London and talk to the King and tell him about the robber problem; all the other towns would send a person too, to tell the King things he ought to know. The whole gathering of men from the various places, talking to the King, was called 'Parliament'.

In the case of student 2:

Yes, that's right. Another thing you should understand is that to be allowed to be chosen, you had to be fairly rich. And it was not everybody who was allowed to do the choosing. Usually you had to be fairly rich to choose (or vote for, as we say), someone to go to Parliament. And you had to be a man, women could not choose.

In the case of student 3:

Try it yourself — the understanding shown in the extract is defective in that it does not mention the role of the King, nor that 'Parliament' was not a monolith, but rent by disagreement. Try to write a brief explanation aimed at giving student 3 a better understanding of 'Parliament', accepting what he already understands.

Now have a look at these following statements about concepts. Try to decide where the understanding is defective and then write a brief 'further explanation' in each case, designed to build on the understanding he already has.

Deciding what the *main* defect in understanding is, is for you to judge. In the example above, of student 2, I decided that the most important thing for him to add to his understanding of the seventeenth-century Parliament was the unrepresentative nature of the Commons. You might have decided that what he needs to learn next is that there were two chambers, only one of which was elective at all. That would be a perfectly defensible alternative approach.

(1)   *Dictator* is when you only have one person for a ruler, as England has only one Queen.
(2)   *Knights* were soldiers.
(3)   *Middle classes* (nineteenth century) were shopkeepers and traders.
(4)   *Imperialism* is when people go to another country and start colonies there.
(5)   *Empire* — is a big place, a big country.
(6)   *Revolution* is when people rise up against the government and overthrow it.

3. Pre-Tests of Students' Understanding of Concepts

Before we start teaching a topic, we need to form at least a rough idea of the understanding the students already have of the concepts we want to deal with. The quickest and most reliable way to do this is to give them a test. Your intuitive assessment of their level of understanding might be correct, but it is quite likely to be wrong. Experience indicates that teachers of young children (i.e. under eleven) greatly underestimate their children's level of understanding. From about twelve up, there seems to be a tendency greatly to *over*estimate it.

By way of illustration, a certain group of history students, when tested, showed a significant level of misunderstanding of the meaning of the political term 'left wing'. To be precise, about half of them thought that it meant something like 'against the government of the day'. Two or three indicated that they had no idea at all. You might like to guess what the average age of the group was, and what, in general terms, was their level of ability. The answer is at the end of this section, on page 33.

Which Concepts to Test

Suppose our topic was the Irish nationalist movement, 1912-23. We have worked out a list of concepts something like this: conscription, nationalist, rebellion, suppress (as in 'suppress a rebellion'), party (political), Sinn Fein, Black and Tans, guerrilla, martyr, propaganda, civil war, treaty.

As a rule we could say that we would test understanding of all these except Sinn Fein and Black and Tans. These terms are very specific to this topic and you would not expect students even to recognise them.

How to Test

The important point to remember when devising the test is that we want to know what students understand. We must, therefore, give them plenty of scope to put down what they know. We therefore do not set questions like 'Define nationalism'. Such questions could produce blank returns from students who had some understanding of the idea, but knew that their definition was likely to be imperfect and so were unwilling to write it. What we want to get are revealing answers such as these on nationalism:

> 'Nationalism is when the banks and airlines belong to the government.'
> 'Nationalism is people who are against the government.'
> 'Nationalism is like being patriotic. But it does more things, like fighting.'
> 'Nationalism is ideas about freedom and government.'

To encourage this kind of useful, revealing response, we do four things:

(1)   Set questions in the following sort of 'encouraging' form: 'Write a sentence to show the meaning of "nationalism", or explain any other way you like what it means.'

(2)   Vary the style of question, using some which call for the student to use the concept in a context, like 'Can you think of an example from history of a nationalist? Try to explain about the example you give.' (There will be much more about the using of concepts in the sections on 'Intellectual Skills'.)

(3)   Tell students directly that incomplete, 'rough idea' answers are quite acceptable, in fact welcome. Never ridicule students' answers to a pre-test, even gently, even indirectly.

(4)   Make clear to the class what the purpose of the pre-test is and that it will in no way count towards any kind of assessment.

Some people use objective tests, where the students have to tick the correct answer out of five choices. These are a lot of trouble to make up, and a tick is not really a very revealing response. The main virtue of those sorts of tests is that they can be done quickly.

Interpreting the Answers

It is important to be very clear in your own mind about the meaning you, yourself, attach to a term; and not to be misled by poor expression. Look at this example of an answer on 'nationalism' – 'It's what people think about other countries.' This does not look like a very impressive response, but, in fact, it contains two of the fundamental elements of the idea, i.e. that it is a set of ideas and attitudes ('think about') and that it has to do with 'countries'.

How many of the fundamental elements of the idea in question are there in these reponses, would you say?

Party political

(1)   'Parties is if people get together to talk on what the country should do.'

(2)   'Parties run the elections.'

Conscription

(1)   'Men in the Army.'

(2)   'When men have to write down what job they do (in a war).'

(3)   'If they went round and they had no more men they might get people.'

Martyr

(1)   'To get killed.'
(2)   'A good thing, like something they looked up to or a person.'
(3)   'Fighters.'

Civil war

(1)   'A war somewhere else from where you live.'
(2)   'Wars between people in a place that are all one people.'
(3)   'When the sides do not want really to fight but still do.'

Treaty

(1)   'What you have to do like you sign.'
(2)   'Signed papers by someone.'
(3)   'If you promise to do something and don't do it that is broken.'

Implications of the Results

(a)   *If all the scores are high.* You can clearly proceed with your plans and, most important, look for chances to build on existing understanding to develop higher levels of abstraction. For instance, in this case, good understandings of 'martyr' and 'propaganda' could be a safe basis for the further, difficult concept of 'myth' as a politic̣ᵃᶫ idea. Terms like 'propaganda' and 'guerrilla', if well understood, might make a basis for the idea 'terrorist' and for considering the whole question of emotive language, the way in which the same man is described as 'terrorist', 'guerrilla' or 'freedom fighter', depending on your point of view.

(b)   *If all the scores are low.* You will need to reduce the number of concepts that you plan to deal with. Also, in the case of the most difficult abstractions, like in our Irish example, 'nationalism', you would probably do best not to attack the idea directly, but go through the move described on page 26, the procedure of writing a simple explanation of the term and noting the abstractions you use in the explanation itself as, for example with nationalism:

> If a person thinks the most important thing in *politics* is trying to make his own *nation independent* of others, we call him a nationalist. If his country is *independent* to start with, a nationalist

might *vote* for things like a *strong* army, or not letting *foreigners* own land in his country.

In other words, if explaining 'nationalism' is really beyond a student's powers, it is probable that the trouble lies in a faulty grasp of those ideas needed as tools to explain nationalism — like 'independent', 'politics', 'nation', 'foreigner' and so on.

We could imagine a sort of pyramid of concepts, leading up to 'nationalism' at the top, with ideas like 'nation', 'politics', 'independent' and 'government' in the next level down and below that level a third level of ideas like 'country', 'laws' and 'language'. If all the scores on our pre-test are low, we might well be trying to work in the wrong level of the pyramid altogether. It will be no good trying to work at the top of the pyramid if the foundations are unsafe, any more than it would be profitable to discuss quadratic equations with someone who does not know how to do multiplication. So, if our test shows general lack of understanding of abstractions at the level we have set them, we must modify our original learning goal and come down one level of the pyramid, at least to start with, so far as we can see how to.

(c)   *If there is a mixture of scores.* This is the most probable result and in a way the most satisfactory. It shows that you have pitched your planning at a level that is neither consistently too high nor too low. With luck you might also get good guidance on which particular concepts to emphasise, if, say, 'propaganda' is generally well understood, but 'guerrilla' is not.

Note.

The students mentioned at the beginning of this section who were not too sure about the concept 'left wing' were in their second year of college. They all had two 'A' levels, including in all cases 'A' level History. Their average age was twenty.

2 INTELLECTUAL SKILLS

We now move into the area of intellectual skills. In the next six sections what we are trying to do is to get students to develop worthwhile intellectual skills and simultaneously to reinforce their understanding of specific concepts by using them, applying them, writing them, talking about them in many different situations.

At the centre of these six sections is the notion that pupils ought to be active in many more ways than the traditional system of listening, reading, making notes and writing essays allows. Students ought to be engaged in a large number of different sorts of tasks, using different sorts of skill, and using those concepts which the teacher wants them to develop. This is not just a matter of preference, it is an indispensable strategy if students are to develop their grasp of concepts. Consider for a moment how subtle your own understanding of the concept 'democratic' is. It allows you to take in your stride very diverse ideas like '. . . the democratic way to settle this would be a show of hands', or 'the American Democratic party', or the 'East German Democratic Republic' without being confused by these subtle shifts of meaning.

At some stage in your life someone may have tried, well or badly, to explain to you the concept 'democratic', but that explanation probably played really quite a small part in developing your powerful grip on this concept, compared with the thousands of times you have *used* the concept – written it, said it, argued about it, read it. Similarly, we must get students to use concepts as often as possible, in the largest possible number of ways and situations, or our explanations of concepts, useful first steps though they are, will do little good.

The idea of 'using' a concept is virtually inseparable from the idea of 'practising a skill'. If we get a student to use the term 'democratic' in even the simplest of ways, that will involve the student in the practice of one or more intellectual skills. Even, as our first section 'Translation' shows, the simple operation of saying in your own words what 'democratic' means can be done well or badly and is usefully seen as involving a skill – the skill of translation.

There is no conflict between 'developing concepts' and 'developing skills' as teaching aims. We develop concepts by getting people to apply a range of skills to the concepts we want developed.

One difficulty about intellectual skills is that there are several different lists of such skills, published in various quarters and using different nomenclature. For example, suppose we put the following question to a student: 'Why do you think Britain did not fully join either of the great European alliance systems before 1914?' This book describes the principal skill which the student must use to answer that question as the skill of 'interpretation', that is the skill of interpreting the two given facts: there were alliance systems; Britain did not join them. It would be equally reasonable to describe this particular skill, as indeed some people do, as the skill of 'drawing inferences', or 'inferential thinking'.

It is perhaps unfortunate that there is not a standard way of referring to skills, but as teachers the most important first steps are to have a serviceable, comprehensible check-list of intellectual skills and a full understanding of the kind of tasks by questions for students which might promote them. When we have those two things securely, we might then reasonably think about adding to the check-list, or reorganising it, in the light of further reading or of experience and reflection.

The first skill we will consider, that of translation, gives rise to tasks which are of very obvious usefulness in concept development. It involves literally translating information from one level of abstraction to another, for instance, from the relatively abstract language of a textbook to the probably less abstract 'own words' of a student and also from one medium to another, for example from a graph to words.

1. Translation

Suppose we have been dealing with the Australian gold rush of the 1850s, and particularly the miners' rebellion of 1854. We have tried to explain the concept 'rebellion', but we want to reinforce it by setting students some suitable tasks. Here are three very straightforward ones.

Task A: 'Say in your own words what a rebellion is.'
We might feel fairly pleased with a response like this: 'If people are unhappy like about taxes and a lot of them get guns and start an army to force the rulers to have less taxes.' This answer is inelegantly expressed, but it makes four major points essential to the concept:

(i)   rebellions are about expressed grievances — unlike, say, the activities of bank robbers;

(ii) rebellions have to be at least fairly big to count as rebellions;

(iii) rebellions involve weapons — unlike petitions or

demonstrations;
(iv)   rebellions have large-scale aims – they are not mere protests.

Also the language used sounds like the student's own – we could have good hopes that this student is incorporating the word and idea in his permanent vocabulary – 'accommodating' and 'assimilating' it, as Piaget describes it. About the next answer we might be less confident: 'The rebels first obtain weapons, then attack police or soldiers, then go on to proclaim a republic.' Although the writing is much smoother, the idea of rebellions having causes is missing and we might suspect (we might be wrong) that 'proclaim a republic' is not the student's own language, but a bit of remembered and possibly ill-understood 'book language'. How would you rate this third answer in comparison with the other two? 'If all the people in a country wanted to change something, like a different king or a different flag – it's a rebellion.'

Task B

We could ask for a larger piece of writing, e.g. *'Write a story about a rebellion.'* When we looked at the student responses, the same criteria would apply as for Task A, that is, somewhere in the story, the four major points would be made.

Task C

We could ask students to *'Give some examples from history of rebellions.'* Again, we would be looking for examples which fulfilled our four criteria, i.e. a fairly large armed uprising with roots in perceived grievances and fairly clear political aims. Marginal examples, though, could be useful to us – for example, in the case of Australia students could discuss whether the 'Rum Rebellion' of 1808 might be called a rebellion, or in an American setting whether John Brown's Harper's Ferry raid merits the title 'rebellion', We sharpen our understanding of concepts very effectively by arguing about marginal instances of 'mismatches' as some authorities call them.

In all three of these tasks the students are asked to take an abstraction, 'rebellion', and translate it into concrete terms of their own – guns, police, taxes, and the like. This intellectual skill of translation can be practised in many types of exercise besides the three simple examples we have given, as we shall see in a moment. It is of considerable value in helping students to strengthen their grasp of concepts and make them part of their active vocabulary.

The principle it works on is that the learner's own explanation, examples and illustrations of a concept, expressed in his own words, are more secure pegs to hang the concept on, as it were, than the explanations, examples and illustrations of a teacher or a book — however apt, elegant and persuasive the latter might be.

If this theory is true, it ought to apply in our present case and you might like to test it. So either now or at the end of this section on translation, you might try two things:

(1)   Make up an explanation in your own words of this concept 'translation'.

(2)   Make up your own examples of tasks you might set pupils involving translation together with some broad outlines of 'good responses' to the tasks.

Further Uses of the Skill of Translation

Pupils can be asked to do the reverse of the process involved in our first three tasks, i.e. they can be asked to translate some information expressed in concrete terms into an abstraction. Like this:

(1)   All the soldiers agreed they would not obey orders any more — what is it called when soldiers refuse to obey orders?

(2)   What do we do call it when a lot of ships sail along together with warships alongside to guard them from submarines?

This kind of question must obviously be used with a lot of care. The abstraction required must already be known to the students and it must be clear, at least within narrow limits, what the required answer is. We can all too easily slip into the situation of, in fact, trying to get students to read our minds with questions like: 'What do we call it when one country suddenly attacks another?' Reasonable answers to this question could be — war, treachery, blitzkrieg, assault, offensive — and so on. It only gives rise to frustration all round if five or six students have to have their answers not accepted before the lucky winner happens on the 'right' answer and says 'aggression'. Here, as always, the moral is to spend as much time thinking about the possible answers to any question we want to set students as we did thinking up the question in the first place. How many reasonable answers, for example, could you think of to this question? 'What do we call it when very many people have to leave their homes because they can't get work?'

One kind of translation involves taking information in one medium and putting it into another — as with *graphs*:

> Here are the figures for cotton production in the 1850s — show these figures in the form of a block graph . . .

or with *maps*:

> Look at the map and tell me how far New York is from Boston.

or with *pictures*:

> Look at the picture of the Samurai warrior — try to describe his weapons and equipment in your own words.

The ability to translate like this from one medium to another is a very important one in its own right. We can also sometimes usefully combine practice of this skill with reinforcement of concept-learning.

Here are some examples, using translation from words into some other medium.

With the Concept of Strategy (American history context)

> Here is a short description of the Union side's strategy for winning the Civil War — see if you can show the strategy in the form of a map using as few words as you can.

To perform this task, the student will have to render the idea 'strategy' into the concrete form of arrows on a map and the like, rather as he rendered the idea of 'rebellion' into his own words in the earlier tasks in this section, and with the same valuable effect of forming his own 'peg', in this case a visual image of his *own* map to hang the concept on. He will also have to solve the problem of depicting visually any other abstraction which the written passage uses to explain Union strategy — as it might be 'naval blockade', 'stranglehold on the Mississippi', 'constant pressure in Virgina' or the like.

With the Concept 'Industrialisation'

> Can you convey to me, using only graphs, that an imaginary country called Fantasia became industrialised between 1860 and 1900?

The special virtue of graphs is that they deal in quantities. So to answer this question a student has to go beyond phrases like 'increased production of goods' which would serve him well enough in a written answer to the question, 'Say in your own words what "industrialisation" means.' When drawing a graph he has to consider, however crudely, how much and how fast 'production of goods' would increase — would the line shoot up near-vertically or what?

So the 'words to graphs' translation question can be useful wherever understanding a concept involves understanding the speed at which things happen — for example matters like population movements, cultural diffusion, changes in climates of opinion — as well as the economic history field where they are traditionally used.

Using the Concept 'Siege' — A Drawing Task

Draw me a sketch picture of a town being besieged.

We can reasonably demand, even of someone who does not draw well, that their sketch shows three things fundamental to the idea of a siege.

(1)　The town will be fortified in some way — besieging places as a military technique is, after all, a response to the problem posed by defensive fortifications.

(2)　The besiegers will be all around the town to stop people going in or out.

(3)　The besiegers will have some place to live, tents or huts — the thing about a siege is that it usually goes on a long time.

This is clearly a useful exercise for a young students not too clear about, say, the difference between a siege and a battle. It lets him produce his own visual image to hang the concept on, as with graphs and maps. Also it lets him show he has grasped the concept without having to put a strain on his ability to write, for once.

Getting younger students to draw pictures is a much-abused teaching technique. Exercises like 'Copy the picture of the Indian on page 3 . . .', or 'Draw Captain Cook's ship' can be mere time-fillers if nothing is being *translated* by the student, if his picture is not illustrating some concept in concrete form.

It might be useful at this point if you thought over this question: What could you ask a student to draw that would help him to grasp the following concepts: nomadic; colony; frontier; industrial? (You might find it useful to extend the idea of 'picture' to include cartoons,

i.e. a series of pictures; pictures with 'pin-men'; pictures that are
virtually diagrams – it is not, after all, the student's skill as an artist
which is in question.)

So far we have dealt with translating from words into graphs, maps
and pictures as a way of mastering concepts. If we try it the other
way round, going from maps, pictures or graphs into words, we hit
a technical difficulty.

Suppose we are interested in the concept 'colony' and gave
students this map (p. 41), of the eastern part of America in 1740,
showing the European colonies. We could set translation exercises such
as 'Put in the main English colonies on the map,' but these exercises
would not get us very far in promoting understanding of the concept
'colony'. We would want to ask questions like, 'Why are the colonies
sited in the places they are?' 'Why do you think the French colonies
seem to go such a lot further inland than the English ones?' We would
want to get at ideas like the fact that colonies are sited where they
are usually for some good reason, or the fact that 'colony' can describe
a small, densely settled block of land like Massachusetts, or a string
of trading or missionary posts like French North America – and so on.
But in asking questions like 'Why are the colonies where they are?' we
have gone beyond asking students to translate information from one
form to another, we have started to ask them to interpret the information given on the map.

2. Interpretation

Since the skills of translation and interpretation are close together,
we will deal now with interpretation and have a joint section of
exercises and summary on the two skills together on pages 58-9.

Interpretation, like translation, can serve the ends of concept-
learning, as well as being a very valuable cognitive skill in its own
right. Here are some further examples of it, to make the relationship
with translation clear.

Graphs and Maps

(1)   'Does the graph show that large families have become less
common in the twentieth century?'

(2)   (With the concept 'slump' in mind) 'Look at the graph of
cotton-production in the 1850s. Was there a slump in those years?'

One thing is clear right away from these two examples – you can't ask students to interpret before they can translate — so obviously we must make sure students can, say, read off cotton production figures for one year before we ask them to interpret the graph's ups and downs. This is the important point to remember. For the practising teacher, it is not so very important to be able to categorise tasks as 'interpretation' or 'translation' precisely. Take a task like this: 'Look at the map of the Saratoga campaign — say in your own words what the British strategy was.'

Whether the task is translation or interpretation matters a lot less than the fact that it is an example of a powerful way of learning the concept 'strategy', and it's a way of using maps to promote learning

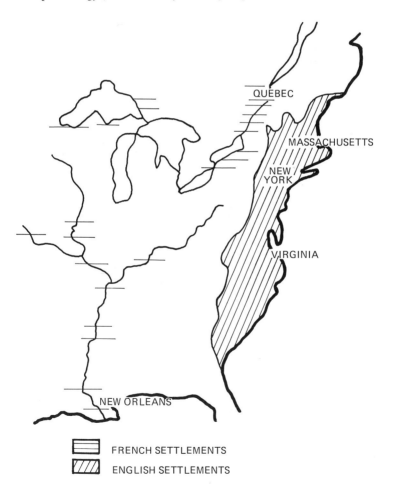

FRENCH SETTLEMENTS
ENGLISH SETTLEMENTS

that teachers ought to be skilled at.

See now if you can make up a good number of tasks involving students in interpreting graphs and maps, with the learning of some particular concept in mind.

Pictures

Pictures constitute a learning resource which is not always fully used by teachers. Close questioning of students about pictures, rather than using the pictures merely as illustrations of a text or a teacher's words, can often be a very useful device for fostering students' understanding. The following interpretation questions based on Picture A (The Death of Nelson) show how simple yet penetrating the technique might be:

(1)   What is going on?
(2)   What do you think the two sailors in the middle foreground are firing at?
(3)   What do you think the sailors hauling ropes near the mast are doing?
(4)   How many people have noticed that Nelson is hit?
(5)   What do you think those people are thinking?
(6)   Imagine you are one of the people in the picture: write a story about what you did and felt on the day of the battle.
(7)   Why do you think the picture was painted?

This last question could take discussion towards the very important idea that pictorial evidence is no more 'neutral' than any other, that photographs are taken, or pictures painted, for reasons — to make a point or press an opinion. This idea might be helpful when considering how to use a picture like B (Lloyd George at the Front) which, on the face of it, is static and uninteresting compared with Picture A. We might ask:

(1)   What do you think might be being pointed out to Lloyd George?
(2)   How near the front do you think they are?
(3)   Why do you think this picture was taken?
(4)   If the picture was published in a newspaper, what do you think the readers of the paper would feel when they saw it?
(5)   What do you think the ordinary soldiers in the background are feeling?

A. Death of Nelson at Trafalgar.

B. Lloyd George Visits the Front, 1918.

C. Tube Shelter — World War II

D. At the Seaside — Late Ninteenth Century

See if you can now devise a good number of interpretation questions on Pictures C and D.

Museum Objects

The value of taking students to a museum, apart from the way it might motivate and excite some students, is that it can help in concept development, perhaps better than any other experience. This is because students can 'hang' concepts on to some very strong concrete visual 'hooks' — the objects in the museum. Let us take an example.

Suppose we are in a museum or museum section devoted to communications. There is on display a set of telephones (see Picture E). Such a display is important becuase it helps students to strengthen their grasp of the concept of development and of the notion that the shape of things changes for *reasons*, be it discovery of new tools, or of new techniques, or materials, or fashions or people's needs; and that old things are the way they are, not because people in the past were stupid, quaint or mad, but for good reasons. If we apply that idea to old institutions and cultural patterns we start to see what an important idea this notion of 'development for reasons' is.

We can use the telephone display to set various tasks. First, tasks of translation. Before they can talk about telephone 1 developing into telephones 2 and 3, students must have a clear idea of what the differences are between the telephones. So we ask: 'What are the main differences between the phones?' (Translation from objects to words, as it were.) Answers like 'The third one is modern,' 'The first one is crazy,' show that students are not ready to discuss the notion of development very profitably yet, so if we got answers like that we would ask supplementary questions, for example: 'What are the phones made of?', 'How are they held together?' — to direct students to the questions of materials and techniques, away from ideas of 'quaintness' and 'craziness'.

The answers, however, need not be technologically expert: a reply like 'The third is made of plastic and sort of more all one' would no doubt distress a telephone designer, but is good enough for us as a springboard for our next question, involving interpretation of the objects:

Why do you think telephones got to be made lower as time went by?
Why do you think the new ones are plastic?
Why do you think the first one is made of metal?
Say why you think telephones have developed the way they have.

E. Telephones

Then we could go back to translation and ask:

> Can you think of other things, maybe in the home, that have
> developed in the same sort of ways as telephones?

Other areas where you might finds displays showing development
are in fields like transport, weapons, housing, furniture -- as long as
there are two or more objects reasonably close together we can use
this technique of getting students to describe the differences carefully, and then try to account for them using concepts like development
in the process. We shall return to the matter of museum objects in the
section on evaluation.

Sources

The use of original written source material is one of the most important
and distinctive activities of the teacher of history. Let us look at how
we might deal with an example (in this case a small passage from
Hakluyt's Voyages):

> The first voyage of the right worshipful and valiant knight, Sir John
> Hawkins, sometimes treasurer of her Majesties navie Roial, made
> to the West Indies 1562.
>
> Master John Hawkins having made *divers* voyages to the Iles of
> the Canaries, and there by his good and upright dealing being
> growen in love and favour with the people, informed himselfe
> amongst them by diligent inquisition, of the state of West India,
> whereof hee had received some knowledge by the instructions of
> his father, but increased the same by the *advertisements* and reports
> of that people. And being among other particulars assured, that
> *Negros were very good merchandise in Hispaniola*, and that store
> of Negros might easily bee had upon the coast of Guinea, resolved
> with himselfe to make triall thereof, and communicated that
> devise with his worshipfull friendes of London; namely with Sir
> Lionell Ducket, M. Bromfield, and others. All which persons liked
> so well of his intention that they *became liberall contributors and*
> *adventurers* in the action. For which purpose there were three
> good ships immediately provided: the one called the Salomon of
> the burthen of 120, tunne, whereine M. Hawkins himselfe went as
> Generall: the second the Swallow of 100.tunnes, wherein went for
> Captaine M. Thomas Hampton: and the third the Jonas a barke of
> 40.tunnes wherein the Master supplied the Captaines roome: in

which small fleete M. Hawkins tooke with him not above 100 men for feare of sickness and other inconveniences, whereunto men in long voyages are commonly subject.

First, some translation exercises are needed, if only to check that the students understand the contents of the passage. They could be asked to put in their own words archaic vocabulary like 'divers' and 'advertisements'. They must certainly be able to put in their own words the phrases 'Negros were very good merchandise in Hispaniola' and '. . . became liberall contributors and adventurers in the action' — otherwise the point of the passage, as concerned with the financing of a slave-trading voyage, is lost.

The concept of slavery could obviously be directly reinforced by a question like 'What are people called who are treated as merchandise?'; and equally the concept of investment could be made very usefully concrete if we asked students to 'Say exactly what Sir Lionell Duckett and the others do when they become "liberall contributors", what their money is used for, and what they get back for themselves.'

Some teachers, perhaps, don't get as much value as they might out of source material, because they stop short at translation and do not go on to ask interpretation questions. One basic interpretation question that ought to be asked about any source material is this — 'What is the author's attitude to the events he describes, what is his likely bias, in a nutshell, what side is he on?' The exact phrasing of the question depends on the source; we could ask in this case: 'What do you think the writer thinks of Sir John Hawkins? What do you think he thinks of negro slavery?' The concept of 'bias' or 'slant' could be brought in directly, of course, like this: 'Is the writer biased for or against Hawkins?'

A second basic interpretation question to ask of any source is 'Why, according to the writer, did things happen the way they did?' In this case we could ask, 'According to the writer, why did Hawkins go to the West Indies?' 'Why did Sir Lionell Duckett and the others pay for his ships?' Again, a concept like 'motive' can be reinforced here, simply by rephrasing the above questions, using the word 'motive'. Or a more difficult concept such as 'exploit' might be reinforced with a question like 'How did Sir John Hawkins and Sir Lionell Duckett plan to exploit Africa and the Americas, according to the writer?'

There are some other very important types of question that ought to be asked of a source, but for the moment we will confine ourselves to translation and interpretation questions in our examples.

Perhaps before we go on to further examples, one important point should be made. Suppose we asked a student this interpretation question — 'What does the writer think of Sir John Hawkins, and of slavery?' Suppose he replied, 'He dislikes both Hawkins and the slave business — you can tell because of his heavily ironical praise of "the right worshipful knight". He comes on so strong with his praise, he's obviously being ironical.' We could reply to the student that we couldn't see any evidence to support his assumption that the writer is being ironical, and that there is a simpler view that the writer is just saying what he feels, and that the cool way he writes about negro slavery, for example, probably shows that he *felt* cool about it — he accepted it. We can rightly say all this — but of course, what we cannot say is that the student is wrong.

We cannot say so, for a reason which has very often been pointed out, that in history we are not in the business of 'right' or 'wrong' interpretations of documents or events, but of plausible or implausible ones, interpretations which on balance have more evidence in their favour than others; interpretations which are orthodoxy today, but may be overturned next week because new evidence is found. However often it is pointed out, though, it is hard for a teacher not to feel uneasy when faced with a fourteen-year-old giving an unorthodox interpretation of a piece of source material. We really have to school ourselves not to 'put him right', not to sweep his interpretation aside (or, equally bad, apparently accept it, but in such a way that everybody knows that we are just humouring the student). We must try to respect the student's interpretation and it is vital that we try, because dealing with source material is one of the few places that the school student can easily meet two vital ideas, namely, the idea of what Bruner calls 'the tentativeness of knowledge' and the specific idea that *history* knowledge is largely 'tentative' — is interpretation, not 'facts' handed out by teachers.

In the next example of interpretation questions, consider some answers to the questions which a student might give, which you would not think were the best interpretation, but which are none the less possible. How would you deal with those answers in such a way that he can see that interpretations other than his own are possible and yet not be discouraged from going on making his own interpretations?

Here is another extract, from the works of Usama, a Muslim chronicler of the Crusades period:

Not a single one of those who have recently settled in the
territories of the Franks but shows himself more inhuman than his
predecessors already established among us and used to the Moslems.
What happened to me when I visited Jerusalem is a proof of the
hardness of the *Franks* (may Allah crush them!). I was going into the
Mosque al-Aqsa. Beside it there was a little mosque that the Franks
had turned into a Church. When I entered the Mosque-al-Aqsa,
which was occupied by the Templars, who were friends of mine,
they told me that I could say my prayers in this little mosque.
One day I went in and glorified Allah. I was deep in my prayer
when one of the Franks fell upon me, laid hold of me and turned
my face to the east, saying 'That is the way to pray.' A troop
of Templars rushed at him, seized him and thrust him out. I began
to pray again. This same man, escaping from their supervision,
fell on me again, turned my face to the east once more, repeating:
'That is the way to pray!' The Templars once again rushed at him
and thrust him out; then they excused themselves to me, and
said: 'He is a foreigner, who arrived a few days ago from the land
of the Franks. He has never seen anyone pray without turning to
the east.' I replied: 'I have prayed enough for today.' And I left,
surprised at seeing what a contorted face that devil had, how he
trembled, and what an impression it had made on him to see
someone pray facing the kibla (Mecca).

Again, some translation work is necessary to check that students,
for instance, can say in their own words what is meant by a 'Frank'.
    Useful interpretation questions could include 'What is the religion
of the writer?' 'What is his attitude to Franks?' 'How does he
explain the behaviour of the Frank who attacked him and of the
Templars who defended him?'
    The concept of toleration could be strengthened by direct use, thus:
'According to Usama, what determined whether Franks were tolerant
or not?'
    Here is another passage from Usama:

I am going to tell you a few things about the Franks and the
surprise their minds often caused me.
    There was in the army of King Fulk, the son of Fulk, a worthy
Frankish knight who had come from their country to make the
pilgrimage and then return. He made my acquaintance and became
so attached to me that he called me his brother. We were fond of

each other and spent our time together. When he was preparing to
cross the sea again to return to his own country, he said to me:
'O my brother, I am going home and I would like, if you will let
me, to take your son and show him our part of the world (I had
with me my boy of fourteen). He will see our knights there, he
will learn wisdom and the science of chivalry. When he returns he
will have the bearing of an intelligent man.' These words, which
were not the words of a sensible man, wounded my ears. For even if
my son had been made prisoner, captivity could have brought him
no further calamity than to be transported to the land of the
Franks. I answered: 'As you live, that was what I meant to do, but
I have been prevented by my son's affection for his grandmother,
my mother. She only let him come with me because I swore to
bring him back.' 'Is your mother still alive?' he asked me. 'Yes,'
I answered. And he said to me: 'Do not upset her.'

In this second example we might ask the student similar questions
to those asked about the first passage and also 'Why do you think the
Frankish knight made the offer to take the boy to the West with
him?' or 'Why did the minds of the Franks cause Usama surprise —
on the strength of this story?' The whole story seems to embody very
neatly the idea of cultures clashing through misunderstanding and
could give us a good chance to help students to make concrete that
'weasel word' 'misunderstanding', often used very glibly in phrases
like 'misunderstanding between nations'. We might perhaps do it
through the straight translation questions — 'Describe in your own
words the misunderstanding between Usama and the Frank' and
'Can you think of other misunderstandings between the Muslims and
the Westerners, or between the Byzantines and the Westerners, that
happened on the Crusades?'
To take, finally, a much more modern source: 'Bombing in war
time' (a world broadcast, 10 May 1942), Winston S. Churchill.

Now is the time to use our increasingly superior air strength to
strike hard and continually at the home front in Germany, from
which so much evil has leaked out upon the world and which is
the foundation of the whole enormous German invasion of Russia.
Now, while the German armies will be bleeding and burning up
their strength against the 2,000-mile Russian line, and when the
news of casualties by hundreds of thousands is streaming back to
the German Reich, now is the to bring home to the German people

the wickedness of their rulers, by destroying under their very eyes
the factories, and seaports on which their war effort depends,
German propaganda has been constantly appealing of late to
British public opinion to put a stop to these severe forms of
warfare, which, according to the German view, should be the
strict monopoly of the Herrenvolk. Herr Hitler himself has not
taken at all kindly to this treatment and he has been good enough
to mingle terrible threats with his whinings. He warns us, solemnly,
that if we go on smashing up the German cities, his war factories
and his bases, he will retaliate against our cathedrals and historic
monuments – if they are not too far inland. We have heard his
threats before. Eighteen months ago, in September 1940, when he
thought he had an overwhelming air force at his command, he
declared that he would rub out – that was the actual expression,
rub out – our towns and cities. And he certainly had a good try.
Now the boot is on the other leg. Herr Hitler has even called in
question the humanity of these grim developments of war. What
a pity this conversion did not take place in his heart before he
bombed Warsaw, or massacred 20,000 Dutch folk in defenceless
Rotterdam, or wreaked his cruel vengeance upon the City of
Belgrade.

Exercises to translate unfamiliar vocabulary are not so obviously
necessary here, except probably in the case of the word 'Herrenvolk',
but translation tasks on the concept propaganda, like 'Say in your
own words what propaganda is, and give examples of propaganda'
would be very useful, in association with this text.

The basic interpretation question – 'What side is the writer on?'
is plainly hardly worth asking here, but there is still scope for good
questions in the second main area, i.e. the writer's attitude to, and
account of, the events he describes, for example, 'What is Churchill's
attitude to bombing as a way of waging war?' 'What is Churchill's
attitude to the German people?' 'What does he make out to be
Hitler's attitude to bombing as a way of waging war?' 'Do you think
Churchill thinks that the British people might have any doubts or mis-
givings about the British bombing campaign? How does he try to meet
these doubts?'

Answering questions like these can gradually change our
perception of this passage, from seeing it as a standard bit of wartime
propaganda bombast to starting to see it as a more subtle document
– illustrating the political and moral uncertainties set up by the

bombing campaign and letting us bring quite young students to a
fuller appreciation of the reasons why the broadcast was made in the
first place.

To sum up on use of sources so far:

(a)   Check that students understand the general context of the
      passage by 'say in your own words' translation tasks on
      important words and phrases.
(b)   Ask students to interpret the passage to establish the writer's
      likely general bias, for example, his religion, nationality, side
      taken in a given dispute, and also to establish how the writer sees
      and how he explains the events he is describing.
(c)   Watch out for chances to get students to use and thereby
      strengthen specific concepts, through translation or interpretation
      tasks or both.

Setting Exercises on Translation and Interpretation

The reader is invited in this and in the other 'exercises' sections to
make up his own examples of tasks to suit his own needs and those of
his students. It is a good idea to develop the habit from the start of
devising tasks at two levels — one for more able students, one for less
able. Let us take the example of the very first suggested translation
task to see what we mean — it was 'Say in your own words what a
rebellion is.' We have not specified for which age-ability group of
students such a task would be suitable; in fact, apart from an
occasional remark that such-and-such a task might be suitable for
'younger students', we have not so far stated of any task that it would
be 'right for bright fourteens' or 'right for average sixteens'.

The reason for this is that fourteen-year-old students (even sub-
categories designated as 'bright', 'average', 'below average' or whatever),
are so varied in their knowledge and abilities that to designate the
suggested tasks as 'good for fourteen-year-olds' and so on would be
mainly guesswork. It is probable that in the case of some of the tasks
suggested so far a teacher would say, 'Well, it would be all right for most
of class 3T, but too hard for some of them — so what about the ones
it's too hard for?' Or the problems of students' different abilities
could come up even more awkwardly — you could set a task to a
group, thinking that it was of the right level and then find out as they
are attempting it that it is too hard for some of them. The big danger
in both these situations, especially the second, is that with the student
for whom the task is too hard we drop our sights too far and say,

'Well, if you can't do the tasks on the causes of the war, just copy the picture of the soldier on page 80.' In other words, it is tempting when tasks are deemed too hard to abandon the whole concept/skill learning project that the task embodies and go down to a lower level of activity altogether. That way, your expectations of the student, his own assessment of his abilities and eventually those abilities themselves get lower and lower.

Ideally, what we need to be able to do is set tasks at many levels of difficulty, but at each level keeping the same concept/skill learning in view. As a start, we would suggest that you plan all tasks in just two different forms — an 'easier' version and a 'harder' version. It is not always obvious, however, what makes a task easier or harder than another one. Everybody has a rough idea of what is meant by 'easier' — most people would tend to feel that 'Draw me a sketch picture of a town being besieged' sounds easier than 'Convey to me, using only graphs, that an imaginary country became industrialised between 1860 and 1900.' But appearances can deceive. 'Say in your own words what a rebellion is,' 'Why are the colonies sited in the places they are?' are questions by no means easy to answer well — they could be well worthy of the attention of an eighteen-year-old. They look easy at first sight simply because they are phrased in a way we associate more with eleven-year-olds than with older students. The characteristics of easier and harder tasks is quite a difficult question, discussed at much greater length in Part 3, section 1. As a start, though, we suggest that you differentiate your two levels of task in one or more of three straightforward ways.

(i)   The Language of the Task Itself. If we take 'Say in your own words what a rebellion is' and make it 'Define a rebellion', we have made the task harder. The actual operation required of the student is the same, but he now has an extra task — knowing what 'define' means. There is quite a lot of, as it were, technical task-setting vocabulary, which we can use if we want to make a task harder, or avoid if we want to make it easier. Some of it is easy to translate into easier language, for example:

What is the technical term for . . .	= What do we call it when . . .
Depict, illustrate . . .	= Show me a graph, or a picture . . .
Evaluate . . .	= Say which was best . . .

Some technical task-setting language is not so easy to make simpler — for example, 'generalise', which would require a circumlocution like 'look at the five examples, say what they have in common, say what the differences are . . .' and so on.

Some task-setting language is downright mysterious, like that old favourite, 'Discuss' as in 'Discuss the view that . . .' A big extra task, or rather set of tasks, is involved here — the student must know what is meant by 'discuss' in the special sense that it is used here, know how to organise his answer in a special way and be expert at guessing what length of 'discussion' his teacher wants. Even more mysterious is the case where a student is given a quotation from a source or from a modern historian with no instruction at all as to what to do about it, except, maybe, 'comment'. Perhaps we ought not to set tasks in this kind of language at all, since they put such a high premium on the skill of knowing your way around the quirky conventions of the academic world.

(ii)   The Size of the Task. To ask the student for five examples of *x* plainly makes the task harder for him than if you asked for two. Asking 'What is the difference between a rebellion and a mutiny?', similarly, is simply extending the number of operations the student has to do, as compared with 'Tell me what a rebellion is.' Asking for a sentence, not a paragraph, reduces the strain on the student's power of organising material, and so on. Reducing the size of the task is an easy, valuable and often overlooked approach to making a task easier or harder.

(iii)   Breaking the Task Down into its Component Parts. On the face of it, 'Say in your own words what a rebellion is' does not look capable of being made any easier as a task — not if we are going to stick to the learning aim of improving understanding of the concept 'rebellion' anyway. But consider — one student's answer was quoted as follows (page 35): 'If people are unhappy like about taxes and a lot of them get guns and start an army to force the rulers to have less taxes.'

To put this answer together, the student had to set himself at least four sub-questions —

(1)   What kind of thing causes rebellions?
(2)   Do you need a lot of people to count as a rebellion?
(3)   What kind of things do rebels do?
(4)   What kind of things do rebels try to get?

In the case of this particular answer, the student has both set himself the sub-questions and answered them successfully.

A less able student might forget some of the sub-questions or think of them in the wrong order and thereby give a less useful response. If he regularly fails in one or both, of those ways, he might well become discouraged and faced with this type of task, give up, say it's too hard — although he actually does know some or all of the answers to the sub-questions and has a potentially good grasp of the concept in question. So, if we presented this question broken down into the four sub-questions, we will be presenting an easier task, with the substance of our aim, strengthening the understanding of the concept 'rebellion', unimpaired. We will also be able to tell a lot more confidently exactly what is imperfect in a student's grasp of a concept, according to the answers he gives to the sub-questions.

Not all tasks will break down like this into sub-tasks, but many will: 'Write a story about a rebellion' becomes 'Write a story about how a rebellion began, what the rebels did . . . etc.' 'Give examples from history of . . .' becomes 'Give examples from the history of America of . . .' or even 'Were there any examples in eighteenth-century America of . . .' 'Describe the warrior's equipment' becomes 'Describe his sword, then his armour' (and 'describe' itself might break down into 'Tell me about the colours, the shapes, . . .' etc.). 'Why is the colony where it is?' becomes 'Is there a harbour . . .? Are there rivers leading inland? What do you think the climate is like? Was it easy to get to from England?' 'Why are the later telephones made of plastic?' becomes 'Do you think plastic would be easier to work? Cheaper? Easier to make different colours?' 'Draw a sketch picture of a town being besieged' becomes 'Draw a sketch picture . . . Where will the besiegers be? Where will they live during the siege? How will the townspeople try to keep them out?'

Probably the best way to work out whether a question can be readily made easier by splitting into parts and what those parts are is to adopt a useful practice we have already recommended and, whenever you devise a task, think out the answer, or a good answer, as well. Then ask yourself, 'When I was working out that answer, did I proceed in stages, did I, in fact, break the question into parts and, if so, what were they?'

Exercise 1

Try making these tasks (all translations or interpretation) easier. Make
sure the new tasks are still translation or interpretation tasks. (If you
can then go on to make your easier version easier yet and get a 'three-
level' task, so much the better.)

(1)   Say in your own words what a Communist believes.
(2)   Depict graphically the fact that imaginary country A has a
large 'balance of payments' problem.
(3)   On your transport museum visit, do these things:
    (a)   Write descriptions of ten vehicles.
    (b)   Make notes so you can answer this question when you get
        back: 'How were methods of transportation developed
        between 1800 and 1900?'

Exercise 2

Devise translation and interpretation tasks (at two levels of difficulty in
each case) on a subject area of your own choice, with students of your
own in mind.

You will probably find it most convenient to think of the 'hard'
version of each task first and then make it easier. Also, you will
probably find it most useful not to stick to the order of types of
task that we have used in this section. If, say, your interest is in the
American Revolution and you can immediately think of tasks involving
interpretation of source materials, then go ahead and devise those first
and come back to the other sections later. On the other hand, do try
to make up tasks of all the types: you may feel that, say, using
pictures as a basis for tasks is just not suited to your style, but give it
a try.

Exercise 1 – Suggested Answers

(1)   'What a Communist believes' is an obvious candidate for move
number 3, breaking down into parts, as, e.g. ' . . . what a Communist
believes about who should own property, who should run the government . . .' etc.
(2)   'Depict graphically' can become 'Draw graphs to show . . .'
Also 'balance of payments problem' can break down in some such
fashion as this – 'Draw graphs to show how the imports cost a lot more
than the exports.'

(3)   (a)   'Ten vehicles' can simply be reduced to, say, five. 'Descriptions can break down to, say, 'Describe how they are driven, what they carry . . .' and so on.

(b)   Making the dates 1950 to 1900 obviously makes the task shorter and so easier. 'Methods of transportation' could be broken down to road vehicles, ships and so on. 'Developed' can be broken down into 'Got faster, carried more people, got safer' etc.

3. Application

If we were trying to teach a Martian about our world, he might soon conclude that the idea of dividing up the world's phenomena into groupings called concepts and using these concepts as keys to understanding was a pretty bad idea.

If, for example, he got a pretty fair grasp of the idea of a 'pen', using the illustrative example of a fountain-pen, imagine his vexation when he encounters a ball-point and a felt-tip and is assured that these are all pens too, whereas a propelling-pencil, which seems to have a lot more in common with a ball-point than a ball-point does with a quill, is none the less a pencil, not a pen. However, if we present him with these various examples of the concept 'pen' at reasonable intervals and in a sympathetic way, he might slowly form an idea of what is central to 'pen-ness' and what is peripheral. He might, in other words, strengthen his grasp of the concept 'pen' in a most fundamental way.

We might in fact virtually define 'having a better grasp of a concept' thus, as meaning having knowledge of more instances of the concept; understanding better that examples of the concept can be very superficially different from each other; understanding better that some examples of the concept, as it were, lie towards the outer edges of the concept (like ball-point pens) whereas others are very clearly within the concept-boundaries (like quill-pens). One fundamental way in which this 'better grasp' is acquired is that we bring our existing understanding of a concept to a new phenomenon or situation and ask ourselves, 'How does this new thing or situation match up, or fail to match up, to our existing grasp of this concept?'

Sometimes the problem is easy, as it might be for our Martian if we showed him a pen similar to the pens he had seen already, except, say, as to its colour. Sometimes it is harder as if we ask him whether the idea of 'pen' applies to a ball-point as well as to the fountain-pen he is familiar with already. The great pedagogical point is that these

encounters (or 'mis-match situations', as Hilda Taba calls them) should
be, wherever possible, consciously arranged by the teacher and not
left to chance.

We follow Bloom in calling the skill involved in these 'mis-match'
encounters 'application' or, in full, 'application of a concept in a
situation new to the learner'. Some authorities call the operation or
skill 'classifying'. This is an equally reasonable name, of course, as
when we offer a mis-match we are saying in effect, 'Would you classify
this new phenomenon as a *pen*?' (or whatever). It is convenient,
however, to reserve 'classification' here as a sub-category name for the
skill of sorting numerous new phenomena into numerous categories
(e.g. 'Sort these ten things into pens and pencils) and to use 'application' for the skill used in those cases where the learner is asked, 'Is this
one new thing an example of . . .?' or 'Does the concept label *x*
apply in the case of this one new situation?'

Here is an example of how the skill of application might work in
practice. Suppose you had been teaching a class the concept 'republic'
by various means and you asked the students to read this passage of
text:

> Diaz ran Mexico for many years, by getting himself elected
> President time after time, every four years. His rule was oppressive
> – the opposition was put down, people were afraid to speak or
> write against him.

Suppose the nineteenth- and early-twentieth-century history of
Mexico was quite unknown to them, you could nevertheless fairly ask
students this question: 'Was Mexico in the days of Diaz a republic?'
What the student is asked to do by such a question is to apply the
newly learned concept (republic) to a situation which is *new* to the
student (i.e. nineteenth-century Mexico).

Important points are illustrated by this example. Asking a student
to apply a concept in a new situation is a very powerful tool for
revealing his level of understanding, as well as improving that understanding. For instance, in this case a student might answer thus: 'No,
it can't have been a republic, because there was oppressing and no free
speech.'

The teacher may have emphasised that a republic is to be understood
as a neutral term, descriptive of a state of affairs in which the head of
state, usually called 'President' is elected or re-elected at regular
intervals. But one way or another the student may have added to the

concept the wrong idea that a republic necessarily entails political freedom, yet he could still have successfully answered translation questions like 'Give historical examples of republics', or even 'Say in your own words what a republic is', without necessarily giving any clue that he had developed this wrong idea.

To answer the question correctly, the student has to match a series of facts against his particular understanding of the concept of a republic. Some of the facts clearly fit the concept well — Diaz was called President; there were elections at regular intervals. Some facts don't fit quite so well — Diaz kept on getting elected; the phrase 'getting himself elected' seems to imply that the elections were crooked. Some facts are apparently relevant, but in fact irrelevant — e.g. that the people were oppressed. The student has to pick his way through this mass of information and decide whether, on balance, the situation described matches up to his vision of the concept 'republic'.

Now, from the point of view of level of difficulty of tasks and setting easier or harder tasks, this is interesting. We can make this type of task harder or easier very simply, and with little trouble on our part, by increasing or decreasing the number of pieces of information in the 'situation' to which the new concept has to be applied.

We assumed at the start that the history of Mexico at the relevant period was unknown to students. But the whole exercise could be made to look pretty meaningless if students happened to know that in those days Mexico was called 'The Republic of Mexico'. This difficulty in finding, in real history, situations which we can guarantee are *new* to the learners is one major reason for making use of games, or imaginary situations.

Before we get into those more complicated realms of making up historical games, however, we should point out that application, like interpretation and translation, can be carried out in quite small, simple exercises. If we have been examining the idea 'revolution' in the context of the first French Revolution, we could ask 'If the French had just changed the King, maybe got a cousin of Louis XVI to be King instead of him, would that be a revolution?'

Here 'the situation new to the learner' is just a lightly sketched-in alternative version of the real-life eighteenth-century France he has been learning about. This kind of question, postulating a change in the circumstances under discussion, and, basically, asking the learner to apply and re-apply the concept under discussion, is particularly useful in fairly rapid oral questioning following up, say, a translation task. For example: starting question (translation):

Q. We've talked a lot about Roosevelt in 1901-3 using diplomacy to get the Panama Canal started — now see if you can tell me in your own words what 'diplomacy' means.

A. Diplomacy is when one country tries to persuade another one to give it something, or really bullies another country like Roosevelt with Colombia.

Follow-up questions (application):

Q. Suppose Roosevelt had actually declared war on Colombia, would that be diplomacy?

A. No, it's anything except actually going to war.

Q.. What if the people in the new state of Panama had had to fight a long war to get free of Colombia and the US had sent them guns to fight with and ammunition and maybe volunteers from the States — would we still say the US was doing 'diplomacy'?

A. I don't know. Maybe there's a kind of half and half between really being at war with somebody and getting at them through diplomacy.

Q. So would you like to add to your definition of diplomacy?

A. Well, you could add that it's not always easy to tell where diplomacy stops and war begins.

Q. What about the Colombians — were they engaged in diplomacy when they tried to stop the US getting into Panama?

A. Yes. They weren't trying to get anything, like I said in my first definition though — so — maybe you could say there's 'defensive' diplomacy as well as 'attacking' diplomacy.

By this kind of questioning, giving the student one slightly different 'new situation' after another in which to apply the concept, the concept can be refined, extended and developed efficiently in a short time.

The 'new situation' can sometimes usefully be an old situation, as it were, seen in a new light. Suppose a few weeks ago the class studied Napoleon I but did not use the concept 'dictator' in connection with him. Suppose we are now examining the concepts of 'dictator' and 'dictatorship' in the contexts of Hitler and Mussolini. We could usefully ask this question — 'You remember Napoleon I, well, was he a dictator?' As long as the class had not looked at Napoleon with that question in mind before, the situation is a new one for them in which to apply the concept.

Looking *back* like this for our 'new situation' to material students have already looked at with different goals in mind has two big advantages; it provides a good reason for students to look at their knowledge of Napoleon and re-examine it — far more useful and motivating than simply saying 'I want you to look over your Napoleon I material for a test'. Second, students already have a lot of knowledge of Napoleon's activities, some of which 'fits' with the idea of him being a dictator, some does not and some of which is irrelevant. So they have quite a rich and complex 'new situation' for application of the concept. This saves us the trouble of inventing one.

The new situation for the learner can also be presented in the form of maps or graphs; for example, students could be presented with a sketch, maps or graphs of some imaginary or unidentified country and asked 'Is the country an *industrial* country?' or 'Is this an *under-developed country*?' and so on. Pictures could also be very useful, in this area. The basic interpretation question, with a picture is 'What is going on here?' The basic application question would be 'Is what is going on here an example of . . .?'

Application and Source Material

We can easily ask application questions either about a source itself, or about the events allegedly described in it.

If we look at the source documents in the interpretation section about John Hawkins on page 49, we could ask the following question, requiring the student to apply the concepts underlined in the following questions:

> Could we call this passage *propaganda* for Hawkins?
> Is this a *primary* source?
> Would you call Sir Lionell Duckett and the others *capitalists*?

The basic requirements, again, are for students to match their newly acquired concept to the 'new situation' presented by the source and say whether the concept 'applies' or does not — or, best of all, whether the concept has to be modified a little to take account of the new situation. An 'ideal' oral answer to the question 'Would you call Sir Lionell Duckett and the others capitalists?' might go like this:

> No, capitalists use money to build factories and things. Well, I don't know, maybe paying for the ships was like building a factory — the idea was to get money, just the same. Maybe Duckett was a

kind of capitalist, after all, only not making things.

(Compare this with the gradual refinement of the idea of 'diplomacy' in the Panama Canal example.)

Interpretation questions can be happily linked with application questions, for instance:

Q.1. Would you say Hawkins and Duckett were *exploiting* Africa and the Americas? [application]

Q.2. If you think they were, say how they planned to do it, according to this text. [interpretation]

Sometimes, of course, a student might turn a question intended as interpretation into an application question – for example:

Q. How did Hawkins and Duckett plan to exploit Africa and the Americas?

A. I don't think 'exploit' is the right word to use here, because . . . [In other words, 'I do not want to use this concept to interpret the text with, because I do not think it can be applied.' We would of course be pretty pleased with such a response, even though we did not foresee it!]

As with the sometimes fine distinction between interpretation and translation, it doesn't matter too much if we cannot readily characterise a given question as interpretation or application. The main thing is to remember this useful approach to a text – 'Do the events here (or the way the writer writes about the events) constitute an example of concept x in action, or not?' – followed, if it is convenient, by the question 'If we have here a case of concept x in action, how exactly does it work out in this case?'

Application and Discussion

'Discussion' is a much-abused term – teachers tend to use it to describe question-and-answer sessions and also sessions in which the proportion of teacher-talk to student-talk is so high as to be not much different from lectures.

A passage like this, for instance, can hardly be called a 'discussion'.

Teacher: Who did the pioneers have to fight against?
Student 1: The Indians.

Teacher: What Indians?

Student 2: Sioux, Apache . . .

Teacher: Yes, all different tribes of Indians. But they all had one thing in common — what?

Student 3: All redskins . . .

Student 1: All lived in, er, tents and hunted . . .

Teacher: The main thing was that they were all living there long before the white settlers. They had lived there for centuries, quite happily and then the white pioneers came and drove them out. Tell me, do you think the white people were right to do that? [silence]

Teacher: Well, were they right to do it, morally, I mean?

Student 1: Well, they needed the land . . .

Teacher: Sure, they needed it, but so did the Indians; did the Indians' needs not matter? What about the morality of it?

Student 4: Some of the, er, pioneers went to dig gold. [silence]

Teacher: Maybe you think the Indians were cruel in some of the ways they fought, like scalping people. But the white settlers were sometimes cruel too. This whole question of the rights and wrongs of the settlement of the West is a fascinating one. [silence]

Teacher: All right, let's move on . . .

The failure of teachers in situations like this to 'get students to discuss' can lead to teachers underestimating the capacity of a group of students to carry on discussion and also to an underestimate of the group's general intellectual capacities.

Let us briefly consider the probable causes of failure in the example above. The teacher first asks factual questions — 'Who did the pioneers have to fight?' He then moves on quite suddenly to realms of moral judgement, but by means of a question in such a form that students have no way of knowing what he's getting at. ('What did all the Indians have in common?') He then states the moral issue openly, but in such a way as to make quite clear where his own sympathies lie and with the question 'Do you think the white people were right to do that?' virtually defies the students to disagree with him. Their silence leads him to rephrase his question, not in an easier way, but a harder way, introducing the difficult abstraction 'moral'.

Student 1 then volunteers an answer with which the teacher does not agree. He is verbally smashed down for his pains.

Student 4 then says something about gold-miners. It may or may not contain the germ of something relevant and valuable, but the teacher does not investigate it. He ignores it, elaborates a further point and then abandons the discussion.

It is easy to laugh at 'teacher' in this little scene — not quite so easy actually to do better at discussion in real life. Perhaps the first two things we ought to get straight in our minds are the questions of what we mean by the term 'discussion' and what the purpose of having discussion is.

On the first question, we might say that a discussion is different from a question-and-answer session in that the students frequently address *each other*, including asking each other questions. Certainly, in daily life, if six people were described as 'having a discussion', we would think it pretty strange if everybody always addressed the same member of the group and if that same member of the group was the only one who asked any questions, or took any initiative in moving the discussion along.

As to the purpose of discussion — sometimes as teachers we are tempted to think of 'having a good discussion' as a goal to aim for, rather than a method of achieving other goals. Sometimes this way of looking at discussion leads us unwittingly to the position apparently adopted by 'teacher' in our discussion passage above, who seems to see it mainly as an occasion for making his views about the world clear to his students and inviting them to agree with him.

Can we see discussion as having clear learning-aims like other activities, such as questioning students? Well, one thing discussion can do effectively is to help make a student feel at home with a concept and adopt it into his active vocabulary, especially by means of applying it to new situations. Look at this passage of discussion:

Teacher: Look at the map here — which would be the place to start a colony? Take a minute to think about it.
Student 1: On the bay there. [points]
Teacher: Why?
Student 1: The ships they . . . the people come in would be safe there.
Student 2: Not if the wind blew a different way. [pause] They had only sailing ships.
Student 1: Well, most of the time it would be safe.
Student 3: Ships in those days would sink easily in a storm, they were wood.

Student 2: What about there [points to map] by the big river?
[pause]
Teacher: What's good about the river?
Student 2: You can . . . go up . . . go inland along it.
Teacher: Why is that good?
Student 1: Trade. Trade with Indians and . . .
Student 3: People in that place . . . er, the colony, the colony would
want to grow bigger and they can go up the river.
Student 1: Do people in a colony do trade?
Teacher: What do people think about that?
Student 2: Only with England . . . or somewhere.
[pause]
Student 3: They'd have to trade with the Indians, too, to get some
things they would need. They could trade up the river in boats.
Student 2: Or go up the river to live when more people came to
the, er, colony. And it gets too big for its place.

Notice the term 'colony' gets used four times by students, once as
part of a question from one student to the group at large. In all four
cases, the term is used spontaneously, as it were, *not* in response to a
teacher-question such as 'What is a colony?' This is important both as
a sign that the concept is being assimilated and as an actual aid to the
process of assimilating itself.

Also, notice that the group are, as they talk to *each other* as much
as to 'teacher', setting themselves application tasks at their own level
in their own language. For instance, student 1 in effect asks the group,
'Does the concept colony apply in the case of a group of people who
engage in local trade?' Student 2 thinks that it does not. Student 3
thinks it does.

Research indicates that students at all ages will both put questions
and give answers to each other with much greater freedom than they
will with teachers. However kindly and encouraging 'teacher' might be,
student 1 was more reluctant to put that revealing question, 'Do
people . . . trade?' to the teacher than he was to ask his peers. And
students 2 and 3, equally, would have been less likely to give those
answers to a direct question from the teacher.

Third, we can notice how revealing discussion can be about students'
level of understanding. On the question of trade, for example, the
teacher might never have thought of putting the question 'Do colonies
trade?', simply because it never occurred to him that anyone might
think they did not.

Discussion is a unique sort of privileged eavesdropping for teachers, in which they can learn about students' levels of conceptual understanding from the world's top experts on that subject – the students themselves.

Discussion can serve other purposes as well, notably in the area of the skill of evaluation, as we shall see in section 5. But we can sum up the case so far – if we can get students talking to each other we can look for three benefits. Spontaneous use of concepts by students, applying them to new situations, freer discourse on the part of students leading to more chances for application of, and general use of, the new concepts by students, a lot of evidence for the teacher of his students' levels of understanding.

Discussion – Techniques

If we are going to try for application of a new concept via discussion, the students must have done some work on the concept beforehand; a discussion is no place to spring a new concept, as our first teacher seemed to do with the idea 'moral'.

General reading on a topic is not a very satisfactory preparation for discussion. Many of us must have set work in this way and suffered disappointment – 'Read up chapter 5 on the revolutions of 1848 and come prepared for an informed discussion about it in Tuesday's session.' An unformed mass of information is really no use as a basis for discussion – far better would have been to give the students the actual question on which the discussion was to be focused and say, 'Read chapter 5 to help you make a case in the discussion about this question on Tuesday.'

It is best to start off with a clear focus for the discussion – a clear question to answer like 'Where to start the colony?' or 'Why did the 1848 revolts fail?' and preferably also some concrete material to refer to – a map, picture, text, source. 'Let's kick around this idea of "colony" for a while' is not the way to go about it.

It is also a very good idea to give people time to think, both at the start (as the teacher in the 'colony' discussion does) and also from time to time as the discussion goes along. The teacher in the 'colony' discussion could have continued the discussion like this:

The idea of more people coming to live in the colony – take a minute or two and write down on scrap paper about what kind of people might come out to the colony.

That is much more likely to get a good response than — 'You say more people would come — well, who for instance?' — expecting an answer right away. If you were to be asked to discuss, with a group of other teachers, the future of education in the Western world, you would probably appreciate five minutes to get a few thoughts together. Twenty-four hours to prepare would be even better. But we are a little prone to ask students to discuss pretty difficult ideas just when we tell them to, without notice.

If students still don't talk freely, there are two main rules to observe. Train yourself to endure longish silences. If you can make yourself sit through, say, fifteen seconds of silence, you may be surprised how often it is a student who breaks the silence, with a useful contribution. If *you* are always the one to break the silence, students will come to expect it of you and not develop what Stenhouse calls a feeling of responsibility for the quality of the discussion. Don't be punitive. Try not to sound impatient, or say things like 'Come on, this isn't hard, just think a little . . .' Don't pick on individuals — 'Come on John, you haven't said much' is well calculated to freeze John and everyone else. Use general phrases like 'What does anyone else think?', to encourage involvement.

If an individual hogs the discussion the formula 'What does anyone else think?' is useful, to get other people into the discussion.

Sometimes discussion is quite lively, but doesn't go the way we want it to. For instance, in the 'colony' discussion, the discussion at the start seems to be going off on to a tack about sailing ships which is not what the teacher wants. There are two points here. First, learn to endure a certain amount of formlessness and irrelevance, especially at the start of a discussion, in the same way as you learn to endure longish silences. Apparent irrelevance may be giving students a chance to settle into the situation, at their own level. Second, don't be punitive. Suppose the 'colony' group had gone on talking about ships, masts, rigging, etc., the teacher could then have said, 'Well, we seem to have a little problem about the bay site — because of this problem over the ships — anywhere else on the map we might go?' To have said, 'Look, group, we're getting nowhere — now try to stick to the point' would be likely to freeze the discussion in its tracks.

Above all, don't give people 'the answer' or make clear by your conduct what you think 'the answer' must be. Notice the actual words of the teacher in the 'colony' sequence. 'Why?' 'What's good about the river?' 'Why is that good?' 'What do people think about that?' He does not let the discussion wander on unchecked and

undirected – he uses two basic moves 'What do people think?' to keep
the discussion going, and 'Why?' (in various forms) to secure full
exploration of the ideas. But imagine the consequences if, when
student 2 said 'What about going there, by the big river?', the teacher
had said 'Yes, good – we could use the river for inland trade and, in
due time, we could expand up it as our population grew . . .'
Pretty soon the teacher would find that his discussion had become a
monologue. Equally, even if he had only said 'Yes, a site near the
big river, now that sounds really interesting' – he would have made
very clear that he thought the river site was the best one and made
it hard for any student to go against the teacher by opposing the
river site or suggesting another one.

It is very helpful if the students can see each other's faces
during a discussion and worth the trouble of moving furniture so that
they can, as far as possible, do so.

As with any activity, students must see the point of discussion,
or they will be less co-operative in doing it. It is rather easy for
'discussion' to seem like a separate thing from 'work', so try to make
the connection clear. We could say, in the 'colony' example for
instance, 'In a little while you are going to have a thorough discussion
so that when you write, your written work will be that much better.'
More explicitly, yet, we could say, 'We are meeting this pretty
complicated idea "nationalism" quite a lot – so we're going to get
better understanding of it by discussing this question . . .' At the end
of any discussion, it is essential for the morale of all concerned that
there is some summary or other written product to show for the
work done.

Small Groups

One of the big obstacles to student discussion is the teacher. As
teachers we have strong tendencies to want to guide students, rephrase their awkward utterances, offer clarification, think of better
examples than they can and generally behave in ways which may be
praiseworthy in other contexts, but which can greatly inhibit
discussion.

One way to get round this is to break a class into groups of five
or six and give them a problem to discuss in those groups while
you sit in on only one group (or maybe not on any). There are some
useful rules to observe if we try this.

It is even more important than with class discussion to set a small
group a very clear task to focus their attention on. The great drawback

of the small group method is that you cannot guide the group if it
wanders off into irrelevance or frivolity. So — make the task clear
and require a short piece of written work at the end of the discussion,
preferably from all members, not just a group 'secretary'. Set a strict
time limit to the discussion, and, especially if you or they are new
to the technique, make the time *short* — so it's — 'I want you in your
group to look at the map, figure out among yourselves where the
colony site should be, with reasons. You can have ten minutes for
that. Then at the end you will all have five minutes to write down
where you personally think the colony should go, with reasons.'

Sometimes individuals seem to get 'frozen out' of small groups,
or even whole groups just don't talk freely to each other. There
are three things to look to here:

(1)   Make sure the groups are in little circles, so they can see
each other's faces.

(2)   Try changing the groups around from time to time as a
regular policy so that if you want to break up a group that just don't
seem to get along, it's not so obvious a move.

(3)   This is an emotionally demanding way of learning for students
— a withdrawn individual could be made pretty unhappy by it, for
instance. So introduce it in small doses and never let it become the
dominant teaching method unless you are sure that nobody is being
made to feel socially inadequate by it.

One great benefit of organising discussion in small groups is that it
allows us to take account of differing abilities among our pupils,
by setting the initial focusing task in different forms to suit the
ability levels of different discussion groups within the class.

Suppose the concept we wished to strengthen by means of
discussion was 'party' (i.e. political party). We might set a basic task
like this — 'Suppose your discussion group had to set up a political
party, in Russia around 1890, to oppose the Tsar and try to get
democracy — plan out how you would go about it.' The group have to
think up their own range of possible activities to engage in and decide
whether the idea of 'party' would apply, say, to a group who
largely went in for terrorism.

We can reduce the scale of this task and thereby make it easier for
a less able group simply by saying something like 'Plan out *three*
things you would do . . .' Or we could use our technique of 'breaking
the task down'. We could say something of this kind — 'Consider

which of these things a political party might do — (1) start a newspaper; (2) write pamphlets for people to read; (3) organise strikes for
more pay among workers; (4) try to improve the way the peasants
farmed the land.'

The technique of breaking the task down, of course, is an essential
one in any discussion situation if the discussion stalls because the
proposition facing the discussion group is too difficult. Suppose teacher
in the 'colony' discussion had been met by prolonged, baffled silences
right at the start, when he asked, 'Where do we put the colony?' He
could then have started to break the task down and set a sub-task like
'Well, where could be a good, safe place to land in the first place?'
or 'Where can you see a good water supply?'

We should always have an easier version of our basic focusing-task,
ready to produce if needed, either in small groups or whole-class
discussions.

Application — Classifying

Here is a list of ten of the policies associated with Louis XIV's minister
Colbert:

(1)   finance controlled by a Royal Council;
(2)   East and West India Companies founded;
(3)   generally advocated peace;
(4)   improved navy;
(5)   founded Academy of Sciences;
(6)   road and canal improvements;
(7)   model factories set up;
(8)   many civil servants prosecuted for embezzlement;
(9)   indirect taxes increased;
(10) external tariffs increased.

Now we could ask straight application questions on this list — for
instance, perhaps 'Was Colbert on the evidence of this list, a
mercantilist?' But we can ask another kind of application question,
which is an interesting and important enough type for us to think of
as a sort of special sub-category. An example of such a question would
be, 'Classify the ten items listed into foreign and domestic policies.'

Classifying questions like this ask students to apply two or more
concepts at once, as it were — with each item on the Colbert list the
student has to look at it and say 'Does the idea "domestic" apply here;
does the idea "foreign" apply?'

Classifying questions also tend not only to deal with concepts related to a particular context, like our 'mercantilist' example here. They tend rather to involve those concepts of general usefulness for thinking about history, politics and society, concepts which often go around in antithetical pairs or sets, e.g.:

Foreign	:	Domestic
Economic	:	Social; Political
Industrial	:	Agricultural

If we look at the Colbert list we will notice an important thing about some of the items in it. Item 1 is pretty clearly in the 'domestic' category, while item 3, equally clearly, goes into the 'foreign policy' class. Item 10, however, could give rise to debate as to how it should be classified.

The debate could give rise to the useful outcome of students wanting more information, for example about the size of the tariff increases, whether foreign countries resented them much and so on. And it could give rise to the setting up by students of a third category, maybe called 'domestic with strong foreign policy implications'. This kind of moment, where students need to modify the categories they have been using and even invent new categories, is very precious (remember in this context the gradual modification of the idea 'diplomacy' in the Panama Canal example on page 63).

This idea of items of information which don't quite fit the categories being used gives us a very handy lead on the matter of progression of difficulty in classification work.

If a student's grasp of the basic classification being used is not yet strong, for instance, if he is hazy about the 'foreign-domestic' distinction at the simplest level, then we should try to keep doubtful, ambiguous items *out* of the material he classifies. When he can handle the basic classification, we can put in the more problematic items in small numbers. We must at this point tell the student that it is all right, in fact praiseworthy, to find items that don't 'fit' and to make up new categories, provided he can justify them. (If John comes up with a new category, the question of whether the new category, in fact, is a useful one, would make an excellent focus for a discussion among students working on the same material as John.) As students become skilled at classifying with the categories the teacher gives them and also get used to the important idea that categories are only tools, not immutable frameworks, they can start to make up their own categories right from the outset.

A useful exercise to do now would be to make up lists of facts of, say, six or seven items, on the lines of the Colbert list, on a subject of your own choosing. Make it a list which you think can be classified into two simple categories without serious ambiguity in any item. Then try adding two or three items to the list which might give rise to debate about how they should be classified.

Another feature of the Colbert list is of importance. The items in the list could be usefully classified in other ways than merely 'domestic-foreign'. 'Economic-social-political', 'economic-fiscal', 'traditional-innovatory', are just a few of the classifications that could be applied even to this very short, slight, piece of material. We can make good use of the fact that almost any body of material can be sorted on the basis of many different types of classification, some simple, some more sophisticated.

First, we can use it to make another distinction between the classification tasks using categories like 'economic-political', the other is making use of less abstract but still worthwhile categories like 'foreign-domestic'.

It also helps us in another, particularly awkward, problem. Very many public examinations still require students to memorise and reproduce a lot of factual material, as well as showing evidence of various kinds of understanding. The kind of work we have been describing, with a big emphasis on the conceptual content of material and also on using the factual material in all sorts of different tasks will make 'the facts' a lot easier to recall. But we will still come to the point where students need, and want, to revise the material in the final pre-examination period. This revision can be a process involving a lot of boredom and frustration for all concerned. However, classifying exercises can help us to make this revision process more active and efficient, and less tedious. We can work it in two ways. The most straightforward approach would be to get students to classify old material they had not classified before. Even more valuable — they could reclassify material according to new and perhaps more sophisticated categories. So we could say, 'Get out all your old material on America's problems in the twenty years after 1783. Now back in October we did an exercise where we divided the problems into problems with foreign countries, and problems at home. Now I want you to look at the stuff again, and divide the problems into problems that making the Constitution helped to solve and those that making the Constitution didn't help,' or 'We've learned a lot since October so we'll use some harder ideas now for classifying the problems — try dividing them into economic, social, political and military problems, 1783-1800, you'll find they break down into different lists from the ones we got in October.' This way, we have students reading their old notes and materials with a clear purpose in mind and yet not feeling alarmed that they are having to 'do new stuff' on the eve of an examination.

Not strictly relevant to the matter of classification, but conveniently mentioned here is the point that all kinds of application tasks that are not just classifying are very useful for revision purposes. The basic move is to get students to re-examine 'old' material in the light of a concept not known to them at the time they covered that material, but learned subsequently. For example, Napoleon was studied in the autumn, *not* using the term 'totalitarian'. The idea 'totalitarian' was used in the context of Hitler in the summer, so for a revision task we could say, 'Go through our old stuff on Napoleon and say whether you think his régime was totalitarian.' (Or 'Was he a dictator?' as is our earlier example on page 63.)

Another version would be: 'Check out the Napoleon material alongside the Hitler material and list what the differences between them were and how they were similar — remember ideas we have worked on recently like totalitarian, dictator, party.'

As well as providing a clear and interesting purpose for re-reading of old material, this kind of task might encourage students to do something which examiners endlessly complain that they do not do at the moment, i.e. to go outside the bounds of set questions and make comparisons between historical figures and events.

Application and Pictures

Pictures can sometimes present a very useful basis for work involving the skill of application. For example, we have already looked at Pictures B and C in the context of interpretation, but we could equally well ask about both of them the application questions, 'Are these *propaganda* pictures and, if they are, what is their message?' We would then probably soon find ourselves in a useful exchange about the point at which a picture ceases to be a mere record and becomes 'propaganda'.

What use, on these lines of using pictures to get students to explore the boundaries of a concept, could you make of Pictures F and G?

F. Children — Early Twentieth Century

G. Children — Mid-Twentieth Century

Exercise 3 (Application)
(Remember to try to make up all questions in a more and a less difficult version.)

(1)   Make up application questions on the line of the one about the concept of 'republic' at the beginning of this section. Make up each question in a more and less difficult version, by *increasing or reducing the number of pieces of information involved*.

(2)   Make up application questions using maps or graphs, or pictures on the lines suggested on page 76.

(3)   Look back at the source material in the section on Sources (p. 49). Make up some application questions (perhaps followed by interpretation questions) on the line of those suggested for the Hawkins passage, and for the other passages from Usama and Churchill.

(4)   Supposing you were concerned with the concept of colony and colonisation in a nineteenth-century African context, can you rephrase in easier form the following attempt to start a discussion, presuming that it has produced a total silence from the students?

Teacher: How can you characterise the different approaches of the colonising powers to different parts of Africa?

(5)   Suppose a passage of discussion, on the same topic, with the concept of imperialism in mind, went like this:

Teacher: Were any African states themselves imperialists?
Student 1: No, only Europeans can be imperialists.
Student 2: That's right.

How would you continue the discussion from this point?

(6)   We can now start to put together sequences of tasks as whole lessons. Here is an example:

Phase 1:   As part of the topic of the American Revolution, teacher describes Loyalist point of view, using device of a dialogue between a Loyalist and an interested, but neutral, person.

Phase 2:   Students work through a set of six questions, embodying translation, interpretation and application skills, aimed at strengthening grasp of concepts like Loyalism (in eighteenth-century American context), Tory, grievance, economic, political.

Phase 3:   Discussion focused by this question: 'Suppose you were a Loyalist in 1775 — make a list of what advice you would give to the British government to keep the colonies loyal.'

Select a topic of your own and put together a sequence like the one above, with more detail on the content of the initial exposition and working out the actual tasks for phase 2. Work in the use of pictures, sources, maps or graphs if you can.

Exercise 3 – Suggested Answers

Question 3. Possible application questions on Usama extract (concepts applied emphasised).

(1)   'Does this story illustrate the Frank's religious *tolerance* or *intolerance*?' followed by
(2)   'What decided whether Franks were tolerant or not?'

The answer to Q.1 is really 'both' – a conceptually more sophisticated question could be:

(3)   'Does the story illustrate Usama's *ambiguity of attitude* to the Franks?' followed by the interpretation question – 'How does it show it?'

On extract 2 from Usama, the concept of ambiguity of attitude could also be applied, of course, or we could perhaps ask a compound question:

(4)   'Which of these words best describes what the story is about: *religious intolerance, misunderstanding, racialism*?' followed by an interpretation question on the lines of:
(5)   'Do you think Usama sees it as a case of religious intolerance, racialism, misunderstanding, or what?'

On the Churchill passage, a general application question could be:

(6)   'Is this propaganda?' followed by the interpretation (and translation) questions suggested after the passage itself.

A slightly different way of looking at the extract could give us a question like:

(7)   'Does Churchill argue his case on *moral* grounds, or on grounds of *expediency*?' followed perhaps by:
(8)   'If you think Churchill is making a *moral* case, say briefly

what it is.'

All these questions can break down into easier ones in the following ways, for example:

(1)   'Were the Templars tolerant or intolerant? Was the Frankish newcomer tolerant or intolerant?'
(3)   'Where does Usama sound favourable to the Franks? Where does he sound hostile?'
(4)   Could most readily be made easier by reducing the number of words to be 'applied' from three to two.
(6)   (i) 'Is it easy to tell which side Churchill is on?'; (ii) 'Does he make out that his own side is strong?'; (iii) 'Does he make out the other side is losing?'; (iv) 'Does he make out the other side is in the wrong?'
(7)   'List the arguments that seem to you *moral* arguments.'
'List the arguments from expediency.'
(8)   'What is Churchill's moral case: (i) against the Germans?; (ii) in favour of the bombing campaign?'

Question 4. Easier version:

(a)   'What did the French do with their pieces of Africa?'

Easier yet:

(b)   'Take one piece of Africa — Algeria — what use did the French have for Algeria?'

or

(c)   'Can you think of a part of Africa where Europeans actually went to settle?'

Question 5. First move must be 'What does anyone else think about that?' — in the hope of getting a more accurate view of imperialism from within the group. If that move fails, we could put some question like this: 'Suppose some African kingdom like Ethiopia conquered a lot of neighbouring tribes, would that be imperialism?' This should produce the effect of causing the students to reconsider the idea of imperialism, but supposing it failed and they said: 'No, that's not imperialism, because the Ethiopians would be the same colour as the tribes', we would then present another 'new situation', for example, 'When the British conquered the white Boers people called that

"imperialism" – how come?' Eventually, of course, you may just have
to tell them that their idea of imperialism is wrong – life is too short
for us to build every concept the hard way. But the rule should be,
perhaps, like this: before we tell anybody their view of a concept is
wrong, try to give at least *one* and preferably *two* chances for him to
readjust his view himself, by asking him to apply the concept in a
'new situation'. (And also let us be very sure that it is a wrong use
of a concept we are dealing with, not just an opinion from our own.)

4. Extrapolation

The skill of extrapolating involves the student in constructing quite
complicated forecasts about how a given situation might develop.
It is virtually impossible to make even the simplest extrapolation without bringing into play some conceptual understanding or other; if, for
instance, we asked a young child, 'What will your mother say if you
mess up your T-shirt?' he cannot begin to answer without some grasp
of cause and effect and of appropriateness of response to a crime of
the magnitude of a messed-up T-shirt. If he does not grasp these
things, he cannot answer.

For older learners, one of the simplest and most interesting ways
of setting extrapolating tasks is in the context of a simulation or game,
so we will discuss first these particular vehicles for this skill.

Games

Suppose we set students an exercise in the context of Industrial
Revolution work:

Think of an imaginary country called Fantasia, sometime in the
late eighteenth century. It's a poor country with no rich people,
only peasants living by subsistence agriculture and making their
own simple goods, like shoes and clothing, at home. The only
man who is at all rich is the King and he needs all his wealth to
keep up his small palace and a few palace guards. (Fortunately,
Fantasia is an island with no hostile neighbours, so they manage
without an army or a fleet!) One day, an inventor from England
turns up, with two marvellous machines, both powered by
water-wheels. One machine spins wool very fast and the other is
a loom which can weave three times faster than a hand-loom. What
do you suppose will happen next? Will Fantasia be transformed?
Is this a turning-point in Fantasian history?

Suppose student A put together an answer like this:

Nothing happened. A society living entirely at *subsistence* level, with a purely *domestic system* of producing goods would have no surplus wealth to *invest* in machinery, no *market* to absorb extra goods (unless they exported them), and no readily available *labour force* to leave the land and man the new *industry*. So any *revolution* in the way of making goods is unlikely, unless and until *agricultural* productivity is revolutionised and a *middle class* created.

Student B, however, answers like this:

The King would buy the invention and set up factories to spin and weave. The new wool *industry* would act as a multiplier, and pretty soon the whole country would have an *industrial revolution.*

What we have asked these students to do is play a small-scale historical game and, by putting the question 'What happened next?' we have made the student use the skill of extrapolation.

The two contrasted answers the students give show us what a potentially powerful teaching tool lies in this simple move of asking, 'What would happen next?' All the concepts emphasised in the two answers have had to be applied by the students in a new situation and in the process the students have revealed their understanding, particularly of the central idea of an industrial revolution, very clearly.

Before we go any further, we could note three things about this little game. First it is very simple. Any teacher could make up a little game like this in a matter of minutes. Teachers sometimes think a 'game' has to be an elaborately worked out thing, in which, say, the complexities of European eighteenth-century diplomacy are faithfully reproduced in fictionalised form. This is not so. In fact the whole point of fictional situations is that they are much *simpler* than reality. If we had asked our students to imagine the inventor trying to sell his machines in late eighteenth-century China, the complexities of real eighteenth-century China, in so far as the students knew about them, would have obscured the point of the exercise. Second, the teacher who devised this game had a clear idea of what the point of the exercise was. He wanted students to show that they understood that inventions are not enough to give rise to 'industrial revolution', and to use correctly terms like 'investment', 'market', 'domestic system' and so on. Games are fun and students like them, which is one of the good reasons for using them, but it is not enough as a justification for using them. When we make up a game, we must know exactly what concepts we want examined and used in the course of the game. Third, asking students to extrapolate was the basic task set, but all sorts of other skills were used by the students in putting their answers together. For example, we noted that the student applied a number of concepts. Also, student A, for example, translated the phrase 'making their own simple goods . . . at home' into the term 'domestic system'. To extrapolate well from a given situation to a future situation, we might have to use a whole battery of other skills, as well as that ability to imagine future situations which is at the heart of the skill of extrapolation itself.

So we can sum up now the characteristic features of a good historical game: (a) it is simple, in two senses: it presents a simpler situation than real life and it does not tax the teacher's research resources of time and material to make up; (b) it has clear learning goals in mind; (c) as well as providing for extrapolation, it gives occasion for using other cognitive skills.

Games and Discussion

In the Fantasia industrial revolution game, we simply set a question to answer, but we could also have used the game as an excellent focus of discussion.

Suppose we went back to student B and stopped him at the point where he said: 'The King would buy the invention and set up factories to spin and weave . . .' We could say, 'Good – now where would the King get the money to invest in factories?'

Student B: Maybe he could sell his palace?
Teacher: All right . . . but who would buy the stuff the factories made?
Student B: The people.
Student C: But the people don't have any money. They are sub-sistence people . . .

In a word, a game can be slowed down and each stage discussed, either with the teacher or in small groups. The object, as in any discussion, being to get the main concepts (like 'invest' and 'subsistence' in this case) used, applied, examined and extended. (N.B. See page 90 for a treatment of student B's response in a non-discussion situation.)

Sometimes, to get the discussion moving, you might have to change
the game a little. This is another, great advantage of the flexibility of
fictitious worlds. Suppose this exchange occurred:

Teacher: How could the King get money to invest in factories?
Student 1: Sell his palace.
Student 2: He couldn't do that, the people would not let him.
Student 1: Well, sell just part of it . . .
Student 3: Yes, rent it out.
Student 2: That's crazy.

'Teacher' now could make a move like this, to get the discussion out
of thus unprofitable rut: 'Well, we could note that one problem in
this story is finding someone with enough money to invest in buying
the machines – but suppose the King found a big treasure, just luckily,
and had just enough money to build the factories – what other
problems could he still have?'
    The important point here, as with any discussion, is that we do not
express impatience with, or contempt for, the unhelpful little blind
alley the students have got themselves into. Instead we dignify it, as
it were, with some kind of summary – even if it has to be only, 'Well,
we have quite a problem there', and then move the discussion on, by
whatever device comes to hand.

Simulation

The distinction between games and simulation is not a very clear-cut
one, but we could give a rule of thumb for our own use. In a *game* the
students look at a situation from outside. In a simulation, to greater
or lesser degree, they play the parts of people involved in the situation.
    We could make the Fantasia game into a very simple simulation
quite easily, for example, by saying – 'Write a letter as if from the
English inventor to the King, trying to sell his machines; and then
write back a reply as if you were the King.'
    Simulations are more difficult to run than games. Suppose we had
a fictional medieval king's council deciding whether or not to go on
crusade. In a *game* if a student said, 'Well, I think the bishop on the
council would vote against the crusade,' the teacher can reasonably ask
'Why do you think so?' In a *simulation*, if someone as it were playing
the part of a bishop says, 'I think this whole crusade thing is silly . . .
I don't believe in God, anyway,' it is more difficult to challenge the
student without implying pretty clearly that you think he is playing

his part wrongly.

On the other hand, simulations give a very good chance for extended application of concepts in new situations and for extrapolation. If someone is playing the part of, say, a feudal king, we can present him with one 'What would you do next?' situation after another, in an interesting and motivating way.

Neither games nor simulation need to be entirely fictional. Consider this example:

[*July 1940*]
(1)   All Britain's allies were defeated – Germany and Italy controlled most of the Continent.

(2)   Russia had to be regarded as an enemy.

(3)   Hitler's intentions were not entirely clear – but an attempt at invasion seemed his likeliest course.

(4)   The USA was friendly (arms; 'destroyers for bases') but obviously not going to join the war in the foreseeable future.

(5)   France seemed to be becoming a virtually enemy power (Vichy).

(6)   The army had lost most of its equipment at Dunkirk.

(7)   The air force was intact and its fighter branch efficient and well equipped.

(8)   It had emerged that the bomber branch could not attack in daylight without being shot to pieces.

(9)   The navy was intact but: (i) Norway campaign had shown that big ships were very vulnerable to air attack; (ii) U-boats were being much more successful against convoys than people had expected ('wolf-packs').

(10)   Civilian morale seemed to be very high.

(11)   British forces faced enemy land forces only in north and east Africa (Italians only).

(12)   India, Australia, New Zealand were getting into gear as sources of very good infantry manpower, though not in great numbers.

(13)   Japan was looking more and more dangerous and hostile in the Far East (Singapore; Burma Road).

Task A: On what sort of basis might Britain and Germany make peace?
Task B: Devise a strategy for continuing the war.

The situation here is pretty near to real history, but simplified just enough to let the learner get to the heart of the problem, without 'real-world' distractions like, say, the position of Iceland, the finer points of American neutrality, or the precise attitude of Vichy.

Competitive Games

Games can be set up like this:

> Group A – you have to pretend to be the Tsarist secret police in the pre-1914 period. Your task is to prevent revolution.
> Group B – you are the Social Revolutionaries. Your task is to try to bring about revolution.

Each group is allowed ten minutes to plan and describe a move. Then the other side has ten minutes to plan and describe a counter-move, and so on.

This kind of game has one great potential advantage – it could be highly motivating. It has two great potential disadvantages.

First, it could be difficult to keep students within what the teacher thinks are reasonable bounds, in the 'moves' they make. For instance, if the Tsarist police said, 'We would secretly poison all the revolutionary leaders' – some pretty unprofitable wrangles could break out over whether that was a possible 'move' or not. To head off these wrangles, the teacher would have to set up some strict rules for the game and could soon find himself involved in a lot of complicated work on forming the rules.

Second, in games we want students to apply concepts in new situations to extrapolate from one situation to another. In a game where two or more 'sides' make 'moves', however, the new situations are devised as it were by students, not the teacher, and so could be trivial, far-fetched, or in some other way not as suitable for good learning as teacher-devised new situations. In the Tsarist police game we would want students to apply ideas like revolution, sabotage, *agent provocateur*, propaganda and so on. But they *might* get into lengthy discussion of invisible ink, pistols disguised as umbrellas and the like, and the teacher would find it the most difficult of situations to guide back to relevance and purposeful learning.

None of these snags has to rule out a use of competitive games, but the learning aimed at should be carefully thought about before we embark on planning one.

Other Uses of Extrapolation

The great advantage of games is that when we put the basic extrapolation question, 'What would happen next?', we can be sure that the student does not know what, as a matter of fact, did happen next.

However, we can get students to use the skill of extrapolating in non-fictional settings as well. Suppose we asked about China in 1945:

> After the Japanese army was defeated and went home, what do you think the Kuomintang and Communists would try to do? Who might help the Kuomintang – who might help the Communists?

The student obviously has to extrapolate from what he knows of the KMT and Communists in the thirties, from what he knows of Russia's attitude to the Communists and so on, to do this task. As with the game examples, he has to use other skills as well, notably application of concepts like political party, movement, alliance, in a new situation. He may of course simply already know what happened in 1945 – that is the snag with using the skill of extrapolation in a real historical context. But on the other hand, he may not and it's usually possible to tell whether a student is remembering something, or working it out as he goes along.

A very simple and useful extrapolation task with any picture showing action is to ask students what they think would happen next if the picture 'came to life' and the action in it continued.

Extrapolation links rather naturally with graph-based work. Students could be asked simply to extrapolate a graph line and, for instance, work out what unemployment figures for the UK would have been by 1942 if they had gone on rising at the 1931 rate, and there had been no World War II. Or they could go beyond that and be asked, 'If the figures had gone on rising at such a rate, what social and political effects might there have been by 1942?'

All the time, with extrapolation, we are trying to move the student beyond the 'guessing' type of forecast, which takes account only of one factor in a situation, towards a true 'weighing up' of, ideally, all the factors in a situation, and a forecast based on that 'weighing up'. To see what this means, in a rather extreme illustration, we could look back to the student answers on the Fantasia problem at the start of this section, on pages 82-3. As well as applying a bigger range of relevant concepts, student A has clearly taken a lot more factors into account than student B did.

However, we should recall that students' capacity to take numbers of factors into account is related to their stage of general cognitive development. So, if we're wise, we start off, whether in a game or a straight 'non-fiction' extrapolation exercise, only asking students to take account of a small number of factors, i.e. three or less. As time goes by, we can increase the number of factors to be dealt with and see what happens. This, by the way, gives us an additional, valuable lead on the question of what makes one task harder than another; in the case of extrapolation exercises, as with application, the harder task is one with more factors in it to take account of.

Sometimes, especially with non-fictional extrapolation, you have to think ahead, and actually prevent a group or individual student from bringing up more factors than you think they can deal with. To take a case — suppose you offered a fictional, but very near real-life scenario like this and asked students to forecast the outcome.

Sometime in the near future, the Arabs, using Russian arms, invade Israel. Soon the Israelis are in trouble and really look like they might lose. What will the USA do?

Now what you intend students to take account of is, say, four factors:

(1)   the importance of Arab oil — using concepts like 'economic';
(2)   US—Russian rivalry — using concepts like 'cold war', 'strategy';
(3)   US—Israel relationships — using concepts like 'historical links', 'domestic politics';
(4)   fear of nuclear war — using concepts like 'escalation'.

This would be a useful exercise. But it could run into a snag if students start asking things like 'Is this in a Presidential election year?' 'What do the British and French think?' 'What are the Chinese saying?' The student group itself could bring up more factors, in other words, than it knows how to deal with.

When people have more factors to deal with than they know how to, they obviously get frustrated and confused and eventually don't want to do the work at all. To avoid this, what we can do is make clear to students exactly what factors we want them to take account of, and also what we don't want them to take account of, especially when we are dealing with 'real-world' situations.

Another difficulty about extrapolation exercises is how to use inadequate answers. Let us look at the answer of student B to the original 'Fantasia' problem at the start of this section:

> The King would buy the invention and set up factories to spin and
> weave. The new wool industry would act as a multiplier and pretty
> soon the whole country would have an industrial revolution.

Student B has taken account of three factors in the situation — the
(presumed) desire of the King to get rich; the existence of the new
inventions; the fact that single industries sometimes act as economic
multipliers. But he has also left out a lot of factors, and so come up
with a projected short-term future for Fantasia which is actually
pretty unlikely. Now, suppose this is a *written* answer, not one which
can be modified in discussion. We can obviously praise B for a lot
— e.g. correct use of terms like 'industry' and 'multiplier'. But how can
we progress with the rest of the work from this rather shaky basis?
It's possible that three factors is the largest number B *can* take
account of at one time — so telling him his answer is interesting but
wrong, because of six other factors he has not taken account of, would
be both discouraging and not likely to do much good.

There is no easy answer to this one: but two general rules might
be suggested; first, retain and accept as much as possible of the student's
forecast, however unlikely it might be; and second, introduce those
factors which the student originally overlooked or ignored, one at a
time. In the Fantasia case, we might do it like this:

> O.K. The King set up the factories like you say. Then one day
> people came along and said: 'Your Majesty, there are so many
> people working in your factories, that there are not enough people
> left to work the farms — we are going to have famine pretty soon
> — what are you going to do now?'

Whatever answer the student comes up with he will now have to take
take some account of the previously ignored factor of the relationship
of industry to agriculture. When he has worked out a solution we could
then set him, say, a reading task on these lines:

> Read pages so and so in the textbook and find out how it was the
> English didn't have a famine problem when they started up their
> industries in the eighteenth century.

Perhaps this point has been laboured — but it is of very great

Picture H. The Normans enter Lincoln, 1067

Picture I. The Fall of the Bastille in 1789

importance. Extrapolation exercises are a very powerful tool, potentially, for fostering autonomy, confidence and what we might call
intellectual self-respect in a student. Through such exercises he can
say to himself, 'History is not just a set of arbitrarily related events,
divulged to me one at a time by a sort of priesthood of teachers. It's
rational; up to a point it's even structured. Given factors A, B, C, even
I can figure out what *might* happen next, at least in a rough kind of
way, at my own level.'

Such a state of mind is obviously greatly to be desired. It is also
fragile: we can very easily destroy it by treating students' early
attempts at rational extrapolation too harshly or dismissively. If we do
that, we reinforce the students' idea that it is no good trying to figure
things out for themselves, teachers will always know better, so sit back
and let the teacher do it all.

Pictures and Extrapolation

Many pictures lend themselves to the simple extrapolation question,
'What is going to happen next in the picture?' Quite often the answer
to such a question might be banal and neither foster nor reveal a
student's understanding of important matters. However, if we look at
Picture H (The Normans enter Lincoln) we can see that the rather
simple-sounding 'What will happen next?' formula leads to consideration of important matters like what exactly might have been involved
for a given city in a major change of political régime in medieval times.

It would be interesting now to consider where a discussion might
lead if it was started off by the simple question, 'What is going to
happen next?' asked about Picture I (Fall of the Bastille).

Exercise 4 (Extrapolation)

Making up games is not difficult — what is more difficult is making
sure they are at the level you want, as to the number and
complexity of factors the students will have to deal with to give a
reasonable answer. So let's try an analysis first — what are the main
factors students would have to deal with to give a reasonable answer
on this game task below?

Concordia Territory Game. This is a map of the territory of
Concordia, in the west of North America in 1860. You will notice
there are only a few small towns. Concordia is mostly given over to
cattle-ranching — every year the ranchers drive their herds to market,

far to the south, away from Concordia, in great cattle drives.

Concordia would be good farming country, but not many farmers have settled there yet, because it is so far away and remote.

Politically Concordia is solid for the Patriotic Cattlemen's Party, which backs high prices for beef and low prices for everything else!

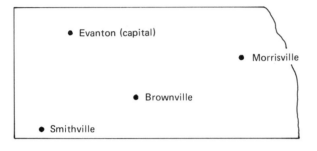

Here is Concordia in 1870 with just one big change — the railroad. How will the railroad affect Concordia in the next twenty years, do you think?

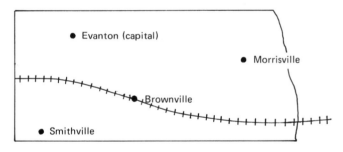

Exercise 5 (Extrapolation)

Look at these written answers to an extrapolation problem — work out what you would say to each student and how you would try to get each student to think the problem through more fully.

The Problem. Borovia is a country in the twentieth century. It is a democracy with two main parties, the Patriots and the Democrats.

Borovia is developing a manufacturing industry, but so far not too successfully, because of competition from abroad. So the Patriots, who form the government at the moment, decide to put big tariffs on all foreign manufactured goods coming into Borovia. What would be the results of this action over the next five or ten years?

Student A: All prices of manufactured goods in Borovia would increase. Some people, like farmers, might not like this — have to pay more for ploughs, tools and so on. They would just have to put up with it, though, if the Patriots are the government.

Student B: Foreign countries oppose Borovia's action; they might try to persuade Borovia to stop the tariffs and, if Borovia goes on, put big tariffs on Borovian goods and start a trade war. Eventually that might lead to a real war which Borovia might or might not win.

Student C: Farmers and anybody who was not making manufactures would suffer high prices. They would get together and vote for the Democrats at the next election and put out the Patriots and change the tariff back.

Exercise 6 *(Extrapolation)*

Take the July 1940 extrapolation task on page 86 and try making it easier in two ways.

(a)   Try reducing the number of factors from 12 to about 6 or 7 main ones.

(b)   Try recasting the problem in a fictional form, i.e. as a *game* about invented countries with only four factors in it. It will be interesting to notice those factors you feel you can discard in the fictional game, in the interests of simplicity, but which you felt you could not leave out of the 'real-life' exercise without doing too much violence to historical accuracy.

Exercises 4, 5 — *Suggested Answers*

Exercise 4. A good account of Concordia must take note of at least these *four* factors:

(a)   The effect of the railroad on the cattle industry (using concepts like 'railroad', 'industry', 'market').

(b)   The effect on the towns, especially Brownville — using terms like 'market', 'industry', 'population growth', perhaps also ideas like 'political agitation' (on the part of Brownville citizens wanting Brownville to become territorial capital instead of Evanton).

(c)   Immigration by rail, especially of farmers — using terms like 'immigration', 'agriculture', 'arable', 'diversified'.

(d)   Political change – using terms like 'interests', 'election', 'political power', 'party'.

Other factors which we could *either* include, to make the exercise more complex, *or* firmly exclude at the start if we think the game is already complex enough, could be the Indian question, the presence of gold or other minerals, the links, if any, between 'Patriotic Cattlemen's Party' and the Democrats or Republicans of the real world, whether the immigrants would be Northerners or Southerners – and so on.

Exercise 5. Various lines are possible on all three, of course, but the following are possibilities:

Student A: We can praise the understanding of the relationship of tariffs and prices, and understanding of different economic interests of farmers. A line to follow up is the apparent lack of understanding that the Democrat party could be, or become, an instrument of farmer discontent – by questions like 'What might the farmers do at the next election?' 'What might the Democrat Party do?'

Student B: Obviously we can praise understanding shown of complex possible external results of the policy. We need a follow-up question which will give full value to the good answer on external results, and still draw attention back to internal problems – for example, 'So the foreigners won't like Borovia's policy – anyone inside Borovia itself who won't like it?'

Student C: Student C needs to get together with Student A! In discussion together, they could obviously have come up with a pretty full answer on the political side of the question. Failing that, the next probe question to C could be something like, 'Who would still be voting Patriot at the next election, do you think?'

5. Evaluation

The skill of evaluation involves, quite simply, the making and communicating of judgements. When we enter the realm of making judgements and giving opinions, it is sometimes easy for us as teachers to neglect the fact that we are dealing with an intellectual skill at all. A skill in its nature is the sort of thing that is capable of being improved and to talk of improving someone's skill at forming and articulating opinions and judgements sounds presumptuous. It also sounds dangerous, for it would not be a long step from trying to improve someone's skill at making judgements, to 'improving' the judgements themselves in the sense of getting them to conform more closely to one's own.

However, students of all ages are daily called upon to make judgements, to evaluate in historical contexts, so we clearly have a duty to do something about their competence in the matter, on that ground alone. And it is not too difficult in principle (though harder in practice) to separate the idea of a competent or skilful evaluation from the idea of 'an evaluation I approve of'. A practical example will be the best way to approach the question of what makes an evaluation or judgement more competent than another one.

Let us look back at the 'Concordia Territory' exercise (Exercise 4 on pages 93-4). Suppose we had set students to do more than say how the railroad would affect Concordia; suppose we had asked them to evaluate the impact of the railroad, make a judgement about it, and answer this question: 'Would the railroad coming be a good thing or a bad thing for Concordia?'

Here are some examples of student responses, all giving different answers to the above question on the Concordia railroad. As you read them, try to assess their quality as judgements, as evaluations. You might even try to put them in rank order, before reading the 'comments' section which follows.

Student A: It would be a good thing – only an idiot would not be able to see that.

Student B: A bad thing, the cattlemen would lose their power and maybe their land.

Student C: The main thing for a territory was to get more people, and economic development. The railroad is good because it brings in people to settle and economic development. There was no economic development before the railroad.

Student D: The cattlemen would make more money getting their herds east on the railroad, but in the end they would lose to the farmers, who would gain more numbers and get rich and get to control the state. Maybe their party would be better than the Patriotic cattlemen, maybe not. So in the end it would be a good thing, just about.

Student E: Concordia would change from a cattle state to a farming state or industry state. This would be a bad thing for wildlife, with many more people, fences, towns and so on. I think this is the main thing, preserving wildlife, so the railroad would be really a very bad thing, although good for people, especially the farmers.

Comments on Student Reponses

Student A

We should not be too hard on student A. He gives no reasons for his evaluation and, worse, supports his case with emotive language ('idiot'), not with argument. Yet his answer has one great virtue, so obvious that it is easy to overlook: it fulfils the prime condition of a good evaluation in that it is clear to everybody what the judgement or evaluation actually is.

Student B

He gives a reason for his judgement, and so ranks above A, but below C, because:

Student C

Does something important, which only one other student, E, does. He states explicitly the basis of his judgement, his premiss, if you like, 'The main thing . . . was to get more people . . .' B does not tell us why it matters what happens to the cattlemen; he just leaves us to assume that he thinks their fate is the over-riding consideration. However, student C's evaluation has a major flaw — it seems to be partly based on a wrong understanding of the concept of 'economic development'. So we are left wondering: if student C understood that cattle-ranching is, in fact, an example of economic development, would his evaluation still be the same?

Student D

His evaluation is the first one which explicitly tries to take account of all the factors in the situation — cattlemen, farmers, politics. To that extent, his is the best answer so far. Also, his final two words 'just about' are important because they show that, unlike the others, he is conscious that judgement involves weighing one factor against another, and so there is always room for at least a little doubt. One weakness of answers A to C is their tone of slam-bang certainty.

D is, however, inferior to C, we might say, because he does not state the criterion or premiss on which he founds his conclusion that the railroad, on balance, is a good development.

Summing up, so far, then, we might suggest these criteria for a good evaluation.

(a)   It should be clear what the evaluation is.

(b)   The evaluation should be supported by reasons.

(c)   The evaluation should not be supported by emotive language ('. . . only an idiot would disagree').

(d)   The basis, or premiss, on which the evaluation is made should be explicit.

(e)   The evaluation should be based on correct understanding of any ideas which are central to the argument.

(f)   All the relevant factors in a situation ought to be taken account of in making the evaluation, not just half the case.

(g)   A good evaluation will show some sign of tentativeness, some acknowledgement of the possibility of a different judgement, even if only a phrase like '. . . a good thing, just about'.

If we look at student E's answer on Concordia, we see that it meets all these criteria better than any of the other four.

It also brings us to the problem that makes the area of evaluation so much more sensitive than other areas: what if we, as teachers, or indeed as people, don't like the contents of the evaluation made by a student, however skilfully it is put together? The emphasis of student E on the interests of wildlife may not cause you much discomfort, perhaps, but it would to many people. And how would you have reacted in the following situation?

A couple of years ago, a young student-teacher told a story to an ordinary class of nine-year-olds in an ordinary English junior school. The story was about a nine-year-old girl in the 1820s in England who was sent to jail for stealing a penny when she was starving. At the end of the story the discussion went like this:

Teacher: Wasn't that awful, sending a little girl your age to jail?
Child A: She was stealing.
Teacher: Yes, but wasn't sending her to jail cruel?
Child A: Not to jail, but she was stealing.
Child B: She has to be punished . . .
Child C: Not jail, but could they have branded her?
Child B: Brand her on her hand so people would know . . . ?
Child D: Cut her hand off. [laughter]
Teacher: But she was starving!

Child C: Well, they could give her food, some food, just a bit, and brand her and let her go.

These children were nine-year-olds — but the basic problem will still be there when students are sixteen and over: are we interested in improving students' skill in respect of evaluation, when what they might produce is say, cogently argued favourable judgements on Hitler's policy towards the Jews?

We might be tempted to try it both ways — hope that as we increase their skill in evaluating, so we can at the same time subtly make the content of their evaluations more acceptable to us. At the present state of knowledge unhappily (see later section on 'attitudes'), this idea looks like a dead duck. It seems that what students will do if we try it is see through the game; reject whatever opinion we are trying to promote, and become alienated from the whole process, so that even our attempt to improve the skill as a skill tends to fail.

The same applies if we think to try a head-on approach: 'If I don't like what they say in their evaluations, I'll tell them so, right out and if need be, argue them round.' The only difference from the subtle approach is that the likelihood of producing alienation, resentment and, above all, *even stronger resistance to your point of view*, is a good deal greater. So there is no easy way round this one: if we are going to try to improve students' skill at evaluation, we have to be prepared to hear and, so far as we can, tolerate some things we are not going to like.

Before we move on to consider the business of how exactly to improve students' evaluation skills, there are two further points to consider.

Judging 'In Accordance with the Values of the Past'

A lot of confusion is caused by this idea, which might be crudely expressed as: 'We can't judge the people of the past by our own standards: their values were quite different from ours.'

In fact, of course, we can. Suppose we asked students whether the sack of Jerusalem in 1099 was justified. A student could reply:

The sack was a horrible event, but to most Crusaders it would be justifiable because they believed they were engaged in just war; the enemy were infidels, enemies of God; and in any case the ideas of the time allowed the sacking of a city taken by storm.

This would be an interesting and worthwhile answer. But it is not an answer to the question, 'Was it justified?' It is an answer to the question, 'Did the Crusaders think the sack of Jerusalem was justified?' and the skill involved would probably be, largely, interpretation. It is not a case of evaluation at all, except in so far as he describes the sack as a 'horrible event'.

A genuine evaluation answer could be given, possibly in this form:

A massacre of civilians might be justified on two possible grounds – that it was the only way to avoid some even greater evil (e.g. the World War II bombing of Germany), or that the massacring force were saving their own lives in the only way open to them (for example: the case of policemen surrounded by a hostile mob). In the case of Jerusalem, 1099, neither case seems to me to obtain, so the Crusaders were not justified.

We want, of course, always to avoid sloppy discounting of historical circumstances, of the sort of 'The medievals must have been crazy – they thought the earth was flat!' But there is no reason why students should not evaluate the events of the past, making their own criteria explicit, as well as interpreting the values of the past, essential though that activity is.

Nor is there any reason to suppose that a student's capacity to experience the past imaginatively, to 'put himself into the skin' of, say, a Crusader, or a pioneer, would be impaired in any way simply because that student is adept at making lucid and rational evaluations of past events in terms of his own value system.

Not All Evaluation Involves Moral Judgement

This point is a good deal less controversial than the last one, but very important. When we ask 'Were Roosevelt's New Deal policies effective?' we are asking for an evaluation, but using relatively neutral ideas like 'effective' instead of ideas like right and wrong.

Teachers commonly use this kind of question with older and abler students, but sometimes neglect chances to ask younger students to make such evaluation. This is a pity. Evaluation is a worthwhile skill in its own right and early and frequent practice in evaluating neutral matters like the efficiency of a policy might make students more willing to approach the more highly charged evaluations of moral questions. Questions like 'Was X effective?' are another good tool in our basic task of getting concepts used and made familiar. The

Roosevelt example quoted, for instance, would probably call for the correct use of at least these important ideas in the framing of a reply: policy, economic, social, depression, political, agriculture, commerce, investment. Evaluation questions are the handiest single way to reinforce by use one particular set of concepts which are basic to understanding of history, politics and social studies, which are often rather weakly grasped by students.

Just consider the mere *frequency* with which we meet 'weasel' words (cf. page 20 on 'weasel words') like the following, in a history or politics setting: 'successful', 'efficient', 'effective', 'useful', 'well-planned', 'important' (and their negatives of course). Then try putting some of them in a context: how firmly do *you* grasp, and how firmly would you guess your students will grasp, the full meaning of these phrases?

An effective President.
Prussia was an efficient state.
A successful King.
Ineffective attempts at reform.
An important event.

Levels of Difficulty in Evaluation Tasks

Let us stay with the Franklin Roosevelt New Deal example for a moment. Suppose, full of zeal for the cause of improving students' skill at evaluation and determined to use evaluation as a method of concept-learning, we put the question, 'Was Franklin D. Roosevelt a good President?' What we might get by way of reply is a blank look, because we have forgotten that evaluation tasks, like any other, can be just too hard for people. Let us try making this particular task easier, stage by stage. Our first move, of course, would be to break the task down. As the task stands, the student has a very difficult hidden 'sub-task' — he has to decide first what areas of Roosevelt's activities it is appropriate to examine in judging Roosevelt and then make the judgements.

So we could suggest areas for the student to look at, for example:

(1)   success or otherwise in getting re-elected;
(2)   foreign policy and war;
(3)   domestic affairs;
(4)   dealings with Congress;
(5)   Constitution;

(6)   how people judge him now.

Right away you will notice a difficulty — that we cannot give a 'neutral' list of 'areas'. Whether, say, 'dealings with Congress' has any bearing on the question of whether a man is a good President, is itself a matter of judgement, of evaluation. Still, if a student is baffled by a question, we have to start somewhere. When the student no longer needs this kind of help in 'breaking a question down', then one of the interesting things we can discuss with him in his answer is just this question — why he chose the areas he did.

To make the task easier still, we could remember from our work on 'extrapolation' the importance of the number of factors in a task and reduce the list of areas to be considered to three or four.

Another useful device to make tasks easier is particularly relevant to evaluation tasks: instead of saying, 'Was Franklin Roosevelt a good President?' we can say, 'Was he a better or worse President than Theodore Roosevelt?' — we can ask for comparison, instead of straight judgement. On the face of it, this complicates matters rather than making them easier. In fact, though, it lets people off the hook of measuring a set of Franklin Roosevelt's activities against the abstract idea 'good', and lets them measure against the concrete — Theodore Roosevelt's activities. Any comparison, of course, has to be carefully chosen. Like must be compared with like and students must have equal information about both parties.

A special point about level of difficulty in evaluation tasks can be illustrated with these two questions:

Was America right to intervene in Vietnam?
Has the Industrial Revolution done more harm or good?

Now, answering these questions would be hard, however much we broke them down into manageable parts. They are hard because they are hard — that is, because our current value systems are such that very many sophisticated observers would find it difficult to give a straight or simple answer. So, although the first, basic criterion of a good evaluation answer is that it does contain an expressed judgement, sometimes we might want to make clear that an acceptable evaluation might be: 'Can't say.'

One last point on level of difficulty. Our Roosevelt example had one great merit from the outset — it was about a specific President and his specific situation. In questions with a moral aspect, unless we put them in a concrete, specific setting, we can end up with tasks that are dealt with in a disappointingly shallow way by students, because they appear far too easy. Look at this example: 'Were the European Resistance in France, Holland, etc., right to fight the Germans in World War II?' The answer 'Yes' would probably be given most times, by most students, after little thought. But look at this case:

> Jean was a fifteen-year-old French boy in 1942. He joined the Resistance. Pierre was also fifteen. He would not join the Resistance because he was afraid that if he was caught his mother and two sisters might be shot or sent to a labour camp. He had known of that happening to other people.
> Paul was also fifteen. He did not join, partly because he was afraid for his family, partly because he thought, 'The Resistance in France does not matter — blowing up a few factories and killing German sentries will not affect the outcome of a world war.'

Who was right of these three?

This one is not so easy to answer, certainly not without using ideas like social responsibility, sabotage, effectiveness, importance, patriotism and the like. It also puts a genuine moral problem in something like the way in which in fact it did present itself to people in real life.

The rule is this then — present those problems of evaluation which involve moral problems in as concrete a way as you can devise. What you don't want is glib, general condemnations of war, famine, and wrong-doing that never face real difficulties and dilemmas.

Summary On Level of Difficulty of Evaluation Tasks

With an evaluation task, to make it easier, the same rules apply as for other tasks, i.e.

(a)   breaking the task down;
(b)   reducing the number of factors to consider (the matters of language of task and size of tasks also apply, of course).

An additional, useful device is setting comparison tasks. Some evaluation tasks can sound quite sophisticated, but in fact be too easy if they present moral problems not in a challenging, concrete setting.

Devising Evaluation Questions for Concept Development

We can and ought to use evaluation questions in most topics, as part of a series of tasks and questions. We can use them in two main ways. Suppose we had been working on the ideas of 'investment' in the context of the nineteenth-century American West. We will have possibly used translation questions like 'Say in your own words what *investment* is,' application questions like 'Could you call it *investment* if a man used all his money in a poker game?' Extrapolation questions, possibly in some kind of American West game involving investment decisions, and so on.

We could now ask an evaluation question such as: 'Which do you think would have been the *best* investment round about 1870 – gold-mine, cattle-ranch, or the railroads?' As with the other skills, putting together an evaluation answer causes students both to reveal and extend their understandings – as in these responses (which it might be useful to put in order of merit, in terms of the understandings shown of the idea of 'investment').

(1)   The gold-mine would be best. You can make more on your investment in a short time, maybe millions in a year.

(2)   The gold-mine, gold is a lot more valuable than cattle or a railroad.

(3)   Gold-mine might give most in a short time, but railroad would be safer to keep your savings all in a long time. So gold for a short invest, and railroad for long-term investing.

(4)   The railroad would still be there if the cattle died of disease, or gold ran out. So railroad to invest in.

Sometimes, though, it is not easy to see how to go for a given concept directly, even though worthwhile evaluation questions seem to be suggesting themselves. Look at this evaluation question, for instance: 'What chance of success did the Irish Easter Rebellion of 1916 have?'

Now this, in fact, is not a particularly good task for developing the most obvious concept embodied in it – i.e. 'rebellion'. To see why not, look at these two responses:

Student A: They had no chance, with not enough men and their only ally (Germany) a long way off. Also the people were not very interested.

Student B: No chance to win, because of the odds and time, but

even if they lost they might make people get excited and one day
get them on their side.

Neither student investigates, or even directly uses the idea
'rebellion'. Yet student B has shown greater understanding of something or other, we feel, than student A, and the question itself sounds
like the kind of question we ought to be asking.

We could get in deep water thinking about exactly what it is that
student B has understood better than A — we could say that he has
obliquely used the concept 'propaganda victory' or the concept 'political
gesture' or 'martyrdom' or 'myth'. But a handy, if less profound way
of looking at it is this: student B, we could say, has explored and
developed in a worthwhile way the concept 'success'. He has said to
himself, as it were, 'success isn't always winning; it can be certain
ways of losing, too.' There is a small but extremely important list of
such words as 'success', referred to on page 102 and what we can always
usefully do, if we cannot devise an evaluation question which goes
straight for the development of a specific concept (like 'investment'
in our first example, or 'rebellion' in this one) is think out a question
which develops one of these central, general ideas —

Was it *efficient*?
Was it *successful* . . . ?
Which was most *important* . . . ?
[and so on - compare page 102]

Exercise 7 (Evaluation)

Try now to make up evaluation questions in connection with the major
examples in this book so far, starting with the Australian Gold Rush
example at the start of the translation section. (Ignore very minor or
obviously unsuitable examples, e.g. 'Look at the map and tell me how
far New York is from Boston.')

Evaluation and Museum Visits

In the sub-section dealing with interpretation using museum visits
we pointed out that one great value of museum visits was that three-
dimensional objects made concrete and comprehensible, in an
unrivalled fashion, the central historical idea of development.

Development is more than change; it involves the idea of a change
that has come about for some sort of reason, a reason which can, in

principle, be understood by an observer. So, with our telephone example in the museum visits subsection, the key question was 'Say why you think telephones have developed the way they have?' Now suppose we asked, 'Are the new telephones better than the older ones?' and suppose we got these three responses:

Student A: The old ones are better, they are prettier and a lot nicer to look at.
Student B: The new ones are better — they would not fall over so easily.
Student C: The old ones look nicer to me, but the newer ones would not get knocked off so easily, so I think the new ones are better.

Student C has plainly done the best evaluation, because he has taken two factors into account, unlike A and B. He has also stumbled on more fundamental truths about the notion of development, i.e. development in something almost never involves just one change — even with a simple item like telephones, changes making for greater stability involved changes in appearances as well. This is very often the reason why a given development is evaluated differently by different people — they are actually using different criteria. If you are making an evaluation of the goodness or otherwise of a given development, it could save a lot of unnecessary argument if you make clear which criterion or criteria you are using and at least show signs of knowing and understanding the criteria used by people who don't agree with you. (Think how much political argument in the Western world consists of one side arguing about individual liberty and their opponents arguing about social justice.)

This sounds like a lot of solemn weight to put on some kids looking at old telephones, but in fact it's very hard to think of a better way of making these vital points about evaluating developments, than through the use of actual tangible objects in museums. So when we plan for questions in connection with a museum visit, whenever possible, our questions should include evaluation questions about whatever developments the exhibits illustrate and embody.

Evaluation and Pictures

Pictures can provide a basis for evaluation questions, particularly when the picture seems to have been drawn or taken with some purpose in mind. For example, if we had decided that pictures B and C represented, in their different ways, 'propaganda' pictures, we could

Picture J. Miners in Wales, 1780

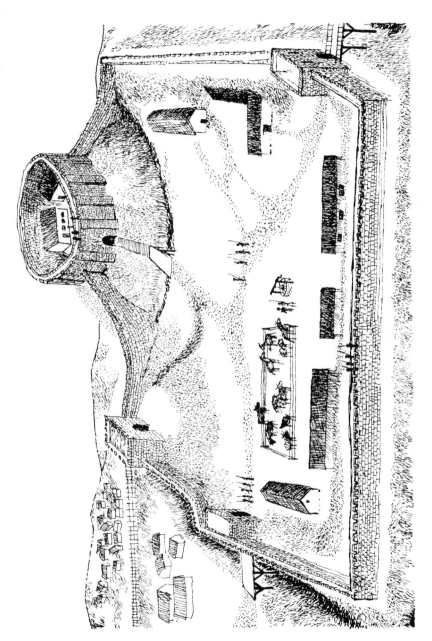

K. Lincoln Castle, about 1100

effectively ask whether the students evaluated them as good or effective propaganda. At a much more concrete level, students can be asked to evaluate the effectiveness, usefulness, and so on of pictures of machinery, weapons, buildings, sites. It would be useful now to attempt to devise an evaluation question on this picture of Lincoln Castle in its early form and map out the discussion that might be sparked off by quite a simple evaluation question.

As this is our last look in this book at the teaching possibilities of pictures, it would probably be worthwhile at this point to do one further exercise on pictures, with absolutely no guidance on what questions or tasks might be set, or even what particular skills might be involved. Picture J presents a lively and interesting scene: what questions or tasks could you set on it involving interpretation, application, evaluation or any other skills?

6. Analysis

So far, we have been devising tasks for students based largely on giving the students the relatively small amount of information needed for the task. When we have given students a fair amount of prose to read, we have been telling them very precisely what to do with the information, e.g. in interpretation using sources – telling them to translate emphasised terms in a passage and so on.

Obviously, though, someday students will need to be on their own with books, or a lecture or a project. They might have only a relatively general instruction like, 'Read and make notes on . . .' or answer this question, 'What were Washington's main concerns as President?' What they will have to do, as well as translating, evaluating and so on, is use a further skill – analysis.

Analysis can be explained like this: it amounts to knowing, in the case of a given body of information, which bits it is appropriate to translate, exactly what to evaluate, what to interpret, and so on.

This is rather a specialised use of the term, but a justifiable use. Sometimes you will see the term 'analysis' used to describe, for instance, what students do, or should do, with a historical source, or with a passage of secondary text. In such cases, however, you will probably find that ideas like translation and interpretation and evaluation are more useful and specific, which leaves us free to use the term analysis for this vital skill of knowing when to use the other intellectual skills.

Let us look at a case. Suppose we gave students this passage to 'read and make notes on'.

The Soviet Period

Since 1917, the movement of Russian history has been from west to east. The capital was moved back from St. Petersburg to Moscow. The Soviet government shrank from contacts with the West. New industrial centres were built up in the eastern parts of the country. After nearly fifty years, Russia's withdrawal eastwards and into herself may be coming towards its end. We shall see.

The Bolshevik Revolution

Lenin had been in exile in Switzerland throughout the war. Now the Germans allowed him and other revolutionaries to go back to Russia. The train in which they passed through Germany was sealed in order to prevent any contact between such dangerous people and the German population. But the German government judged that it was in their interest that Lenin should be in Russia and at liberty, for he was the leader of the only political party which was in favour of peace with Germany at almost any price.

The mass of the Russian people wanted two things, peace and land. The Mensheviks and SRs were in the Provisional Government, and they wanted peace, but not at the price of a German victory. They believed that if the Kaiser's Germany won, the Russian Revolution would soon be finished. A majority of the Provisional Government wanted the peasants to get most of the land, but they insisted that this must be done by due process of law and that meant delay. Moreover, the Russian peasant's experience of law was that it usually ended by cheating peasants.

The Bolsheviks, also called Communists, were not in the government, and they had no difficulty in outbidding the other parties. They had no use for legal forms, they said 'Let the peasants take the land at once.' They were prepared to risk a German victory; so they could also promise peace at once. They believed that in any case no socialist revolution could survive in Russia unless it spread to other lands, and also that there would soon be a Communist revolution in Germany. Events showed that both these calculations were wrong, but that did not effect the immediate issue.

J. Lawrence, *Russia*, Methuen, 1965.

Normally, of course, teachers would set much longer passages for students to read but this piece will serve to illustrate the point. Now, suppose we have given the students this task: 'Make notes about why Lenin and the Germans co-operated in 1917.' This will direct their work much more usefully than just saying 'make notes' — but it still leaves them a lot of analysis to do. Here are just a few of the sub-tasks they have to analyse that basic task into.

Translation

They have to recognise that they ought to translate into their own words, either in their heads or actually in their written notes, terms like:

(1)   movement of Russian history has been from west to east;
(2)   Soviet government shrank from contact with the West;
(3)   such dangerous people;
(4)   due process of law — and others.

Interpretation

They have to set themselves, and then answer, this interpretation question — 'Why, in the author's view, did the Germans help Lenin — and why did Lenin go along with them?'

Evaluation

All items of information have to be evaluated from the point of view of their relevance and importance to answering the main question. In the first paragraph, for example, the student must make a judgement about whether anything in the paragraph is important at all in answering this question.

Application

The student has to decide whether and how the concept 'co-operation' applies to the relationships of Lenin and the Germans.

Now, clearly, a student might analyse the task correctly and still do badly. He might give poor translations, wrong interpretation, and so on. At least we would know exactly where he was going wrong, and be able to help him. But how would a student's work look if he was failing to do the analysis itself properly for this particular task?

The grossest way he could show failure to analyse would be to copy down all, or long bits of, the passage verbatim. All teachers have seen students, even college students, act in this way when they fail to analyse well.

Or he might do some of the analysis correctly, but not enough of it.

Look at this response, for example:

Student A (notes):
(1)   Russia cut itself off from 1917.
(2)   New industrial cities built in East.
(3)   Lenin in Switzerland 1914 to 1917.
(4)   Train sealed through Germany.
(5)   Mensheviks in Provisional Government, also SRs.
(6)   Provisional Government, wants peasants have land.
(7)   Bolsheviks also called Communist.
(8)   Thought there would soon be a revolution in Germany.

Again, all teachers have seen work like this. Faced with this kind of thing, it is easy to feel confused about what to say to a student, not know where to start, and finish up with some lame and unhelpful advice like 'Try to be more relevant' or even 'Think harder'.

However, using the idea of analysis, it might be possible to describe more constructively where the student has gone wrong. Let us try to work out how well or badly he has analysed the task and the material.

(1)   *Has he translated where appropriate?* Sometimes, at least, he has. He translated, for example, from the highly abstract '. . . the movement of Russian history . . . contacts with the West' correctly into the simpler idea '. . . cut itself off'.

(2)   *Has he interpreted where appropriate?* Clearly not — there is no indication of what he thinks the author's view of the question might be, it is not even clear that he thinks the author has a view at all, from the notes.

(3)   *Does he evaluate?* Well, he may have done. He may really think that the eight points he gives us actually are the most important items, in which case he has simply made a bad, hard-to-defend evaluation. On the other hand, the way he has spread the points evenly, taking two points from each paragraph, might indicate that he is not clear that he should be evaluating the information by the criteria of relevance and importance.

(4)   Similarly, the failure to interpret the author's view brings in its train a failure to consider the *application* of the concept 'co-operation' in this context.

The importance of being able to analyse properly is pretty obvious from this cursory look at this student's work. If we do not know when it is appropriate to translate things, or evaluate, and all the other processes, then using a book or lecture as an information source becomes very difficult. Our notebooks become useless to us: imagine student A coming back to these notes after six months and trying to use them to make sense of the relations of Lenin and the Germans in 1917!

So, how could we help student A to improve? First, we could apply our two simple principles: make the task smaller and break the task down. We could set shorter passages of reading to students having difficulty making notes on books, or in the case of the Lenin/German question ask only half the question, i.e. 'Make notes on why Germany helped Lenin in 1917.'

Also, of course, we could avoid the analysis task altogether, if we chose, by setting very specific tasks – 'Read the passage and say in your own words what the following words mean . . . say why the writer thinks Lenin went along with the Germans . . . list the three most important points the writer makes and say why they are important', and so on.

That is all right where a student really cannot handle analysis and you need to get on. But we should realise that if we do that, we are just putting off the problem, and that admirable and useful as the specific tasks are, someday a student will be in the position of needing to do his own analysis.

More positively, we can do three simple but helpful things.

We can give students models. We could, for instance, give a model of good notes on the Lenin/German co-operation, like this perhaps:

(1)   Lenin in Switzerland 1914-17.

(2)   Germans in 1917 let him go to Russia through Germany.

(3)   Germans did not want him to talk Communism to German people, so train sealed.

(4)   Germans wanted Lenin to win in Russia because Lenin would make peace with Germany if he got in power.

(5)   Lenin did not mind stopping the war even if Germans profited. Thought there would be revolution soon in Germany anyway. Other people in Russia were scared Germany would stop Russian revolution if she won war.

(6)   Germany-Lenin not allies like Germany-Austria; did not really like each other at all but only 'co-operated' for time being.

We could now go through the example with students and make the

most important move towards improving students' skill at analysis,
i.e. *make explicit what is required of them.* Our explanation might be:

> Notice first how my notes are in my own simple words. Always
> try to use your own words in notes; never just copy down a phrase
> just because it sounds good. Never put down anything you don't
> understand. If you come to something important in hard language,
> try to explain it in your own language.
>
> Second, notice how in points 3 and 4 and 5 I try to answer the
> question set, 'Why Lenin and the Germans were co-operating in
> 1917', just like in an essay. Notes ought to try to answer the
> questions, like you do in essays.
>
> Third, notice how I don't have any notes at all on that first
> paragraph. That's because I judged it was not important for
> answering the question. All the time when you read things in the
> book, you have to *judge*: 'Is this important to the question?' If you
> think it is not, leave it out. Sometimes there might be a whole
> page you want to leave out. If you like, you can show me you have
> not just forgotten to read that page – you can put in your notes
> – 'page 12 – nothing important on that page', or even 'page 12 –
> a lot of stuff about the Duma – not sure how it's important, so I
> left it out.' I won't mind if you are wrong, just so long as you are
> *trying* to judge what's important.
>
> These are the three main things you always should do making
> notes – use your own words (translate), say what the book's opinion
> on the set question is (interpret), and judge which parts are
> important and which not (evaluate).
>
> There was another thing I did in point 5 – I compared this bit
> of history with another bit and said how it was different – in this
> case how 'co-operate' meant something a bit different with Lenin
> and Germany from what it could mean talking about Germany and
> Austria. You can't always do this with notes, but you can some-
> times, and it's a good thing to do if you can.

So we can give models and we can try to give explanations of
what we want. The third thing we can do has already been briefly
referred to, and the necessity for it is obvious from the suggested
explanations of note-taking to students. That explanation refers
more than once to 'the question', i.e. 'Why were Lenin and the
Germans co-operating?' Whenever students set out to acquire
information through note-taking, they ought to have a focusing

question. They could be given it by the teacher, or make it up themselves, but a question of some kind they must have.

Before we move on, we should now consolidate a little: with each of the following extracts, try to do two things:

(a)   Make up a question for students to use to focus a note-taking task. Remember to keep the question short: do not do the whole analysis task for them.

(b)   Draw up a set of model notes on the passage to illustrate to students three main aspects of note-taking — translation, interpretation and evaluation.

The Inter-War Period, 1921-39

In the Treaty of Lausanne of 1923 which established the independence of Nationalist Turkey and regulated her relations with the Western Powers, she had to concede the demilitarisation of the Zone of the Straits: the warships of all nations, with slight restrictions, were free to enter the Black Sea. This was obnoxious not only to Turkey, as limiting her sovereignty, but also to Russia, as exposing her Black Sea coast to the threat of an enemy navy, and in 1925, while Turkey was involved in the acute dispute with Britain and Iraq over the possession of the villayet of Mosal, Russia concluded with her a new Treaty of Friendship and Neutrality. Though official relations between Russia and Turkey remained cordial, and the Russians gave more technical help with the industrialisation of Turkey, there was little contact or cultural interchange between the two people. The Turkish dictatorship permitted the works of Marx and Lenin to be read, but imprisoned active Communists under laws which forbade associations with the purpose of propagating ideas of class distinction, or of class conflict, or with internationalist intentions.

In 1936, when Italy had emerged as the aggressive naval power which threatened the *status quo* in the Mediterranean, Turkey proposed to the signatories of the Treaty of Lausanne that the régime of the Straits needed revision, and obtained important concessions in the Montreux Convention. She was now allowed to fortify the Straits, and in time of war to close them to the warships of all Powers, unless acting under the Covenant of the League of Nations.

G.E. Kirk,
A Short History of the Middle East, Methuen, 1964

No account of twelfth-century English commerce would be
complete without mention of the Jews, who formed another
community of 'foreign' merchants, as important in their own
specialisation, money-lending, as were the Italians or Flemings in
the wool trade. To lend money at interest ran counter to the
teaching of Canon Law, and in Northern Europe, where the
influence of the Church was not tempered by any secular com-
mercial traditions, Christians could not practise usury, though they
had begun to see its advantages. This need was therefore met by
small groups of Jewish financiers, tolerated rather than welcomed
because of the services they could render to kings, barons and
even Churches in want of ready money. Successful Jews became
extremely wealthy and as such doubly the object of popular envy
and hatred. Legally they were counted personal serfs of the King,
and so long as he protected them, they were secure. But when
that protection failed, they were liable to become victims of savage
outbursts of mass-hysteria: at York, for example, on Henry II's
death in 1189, some local barons in debt to the Jews incited a
city mob to murder a large number of them and pillage their houses.
Yet if it had not been for the Jews, many enterprises requiring large
amounts of capital, especially the construction of some of the great
Cathedrals and monastic Churches, could hardly have been carried
through. By the end of the thirteenth century, Christians had
found it possible to engage in usury without cost to their con-
sciences, and in 1290 Edward I actually expelled all the Jews from
England, a small and unlamented community which had first
attained much wealth, had then suffered prolonged persecution,
and had finally, in the Crown's view, outlived its usefulness.

G.W.S. Barrow,
Feudal Britain, Edward Arnold, 1956.

The Western Allies held democratic elections as early as 1946, to
elect parliaments for the *Lander*. The rebuilding of the physical
and moral ruin of German education was put in hand, and the
teaching profession was purged of Nazis, perhaps more thoroughly
than any other. New textbooks, free of the distorted fantasies of
National Socialism, were rapidly produced.

The Allies divided the Nazis' single trade union into twelve new
unions, with a simplified union structure. Most important, the
Western Allies encouraged the growth of a free press reflecting
many shades of opinion. Finally, a limited number of industries

with export potential were started up under military guidance.

The Western Allies governed Germany during the years of the worst shortages and difficulties and gave the Germans time to recover before they tried, once more, to govern themselves demo-cratically. The prime movers in this were the Americans. Whether they were motivated more by a genuine love of democracy, or by a fear of Stalinist Communism, it is impossible to say. The British in any case agreed with them, and the French were too weak to oppose them.

Germany, 1870-1970, R. Morgan (ed.),
BBC Publications, 1970.

In the great wars between the French and the English for the control of North America, no tribe played a more important role than did the Iroquois of central New York. When the French came into the St. Lawrence Valley the Iroquois felt threatened. For a time the Iroquois had forced the Algonquins and Hurons to accept their supremacy. Now these subject tribes preferred to sell their furs directly to the French rather than to let the Iroquois control their trade with the white man. In short the Iroquois and the French hit it off badly from the start.

In 1609 the great French explorer Champlain invaded the Iroquois country on the lake that bears his name. Fighting between French and Iroquois broke out. In 1615 Champlain's men attacked an Onondaga village. This was fortified. There was a moat or ditch filled with water which ran round the village and a double wall or stockade. But the white men built a platform and moved close to the walls. Then from the platform they could shoot over the stockade and bring terror and death to the defenders. The village was soon taken. So began a long enmity between the Iroquois and the French. This was to cost the French their empire in America.

The Iroquois turned to the Dutch for arms, and got them. They then set out to capture the rich fur trade of the interior of the country. The Hurons and Algonquins controlled that trade, and the Iroquois planned to smash their rivals.

Morris, *First Book of the Indian Wars*,
Franklin Watts, 1959

Pre-Tests of Skill of Analysis

With a new group of students, it would be very useful to have a rough idea of their ability to use the analysis skills involved in making notes —

as desirable, in fact, as having knowledge of their conceptual levels.

The students ought to be tested on their capacity both to make notes from books and to make notes on information given orally by the teacher. As making notes is such a common activity in schools, you probably need not even announce that the tests are tests at all. It would be a good idea, though, to announce that you intend to take the notes in to look at them and that sometimes you might give them a mark. A very useful preliminary move in trying to improve the quality of note-taking is to impress on students that notes are important pieces of writing, which can be judged bad or good like other pieces of writing. The simplest way to establish this point, of course, is to take notes in and mark and comment on them from time to time.

Analysis and Source-Materials

The analysis operation that a student has to perform on a piece of historical source material is similar to the operation he does on, say, a history textbook, but more complicated. For example, consider this passage where the student has been given the focusing question, 'What were the nineteenth-century Chinese like?'

A European in Nineteenth-Century China

In their diversions, the Chinese have much of that childish character which distinguishes other Asiatics . . . The childish mind under a despotism has few of those calls for exertion, among the bulk of the people, which in free states give it manly strength and vigour. Bearing no part in public transactions, and living in un-interrupted peace, the uniform insipidity of their existence is relieved by any, even the most frivolous and puerile, amusements . . . My attention was drawn by several old Chinese, some of whom had grey beards, and nearly all of them huge goggling spectacles. A few were chirruping and chuckling to singing-birds, which they carried in bamboo cages, or perched on a stick; others were catching flies to feed the birds: the remainder of the party seemed to be delightedly employed in flying paper kites, while a group of boys were gravely looking on, and regarding these innocent occupations of their seniors with the most serious and gratified attention.

J.F. Davis, *The Chinese*, 1854,
quoted in K. Pratt, *Visitors to China*,
Macmillan, 1968.

As with any information-gathering, note-taking task, the student will have to analyse:

> which terms he has to translate (e.g. 'public transactions');
> which parts are important and relevant (evaluation) to the question;
> which parts show the writer's view (i.e. interpretation).

Obviously, though, it's not as simple as that. It is pretty clear from this passage that the nineteenth-century Chinese were infantile and they were that way because they lived under a despotism. Equally clearly, that is merely this writer's idiosyncratic opinion.

What students have to do, as well as the three moves listed above, is analyse which parts are relevant and important: (a) to answering the question ('What were nineteenth-century Chinese like?'); and (b) to revealing the writer's point of view about the question. Even before he starts doing that, he must have answered this application question: 'Is this passage a "primary source"?, i.e. the kind of material where I have to take very particular note of the writer's angle on events, as well as of the events themselves.' If he decides that it is indeed a 'primary source' he might well decide also to set himself further application tasks at certain appropriate points, i.e. applying concepts used generally to describe writer's attitudes, such as bias, neutral, tolerant, nationalistic and so on.

Any attempt by students to use source material in which they do not perform these analysis operations will probably yield nonsense by way of notes. Students should have a lot of practice in highly structured and guided work with sources (see section on interpretation using sources) before they are asked to deal with them in a less teacher-controlled way, as in project work, for instance.

Project Work

We have referred more than once to 'project work'. It is time to look at it in more detail.

What makes a project a project is the way the teacher sets it up. Thus, if a teacher says, 'Here's a little book about Columbus – find out about Columbus from it – I'll check with you in thirty minutes', he has in fact set the student a miniature *project*.

It is a very small project, but a genuine one, because the teacher has designated only a general area of work, not a specific task or tasks. Analysing that area of work into a series of specific tasks to do, concepts to master, and so on, is left to the student. That is the distinctive feature of a 'project'.

Projects can differ greatly in size, time allotted for them, whether they are for individuals or for groups, whether teachers prescribe in detail what books and material to use, or just say, 'The library's that way . . .' They can differ greatly in the kind of end product they have in view, whether a written thesis, a display, a tape-recording, a slide-sequence or whatever. But they all have this in common — that the student must come up with his own specific questions and tasks, by a process of analysis.

When projects go wrong, it is usually because this analysis has been poor, or not done at all. So we get the mass of factual information, the unrelated pictures, the whole sad waste of effort characteristic of the project that did not work out.

There are two main reasons for using project work. First, it is popular as a form of work, with most students, partly for good, and partly for bad, reasons. The good reasons are that many students like the feeling of being able to organise a big piece of work independently — even if they are not doing it very well. Many students also are interested and motivated by the elements of novelty in project work — the sheer size of the enterprise and the end product, compared to a standard piece of class-work; the unusual kind of end product, such as displays; the element of co-operating with other students, if it is a group project. The bad reasons are interesting too because, perhaps, there can be satisfaction arising precisely from the fact that the necessary analysis has not been done. If a student has spent a lot of the time answering that kind of pointed, searching question advocated in this book — 'What does x mean?' 'How would you evaluate y?' — then it can be a relief to spend time quietly paraphrasing, or even copying, some book about the Aztecs, with no tiresome *task* to think about, no difficult thinking to do at all — and at the end of it, a large, satisfying end product. To follow this point through would get us into some pretty deep water. Perhaps it is enough to say that it is only realistic to recognise that not all students get their satisfactions in school-work from useful thinking. So a student who is happily employed on a project is not necessarily well employed. It would be equally foolish, though, to ignore the good reasons students have for liking project work, and the powerful motivation tool that might put in our hands.

The second main argument for project work is this: it can be an excellent way of developing the skill of analysis and, in later life, after school, that skill will be the key to the successful use of all the other cognitive skills. In adult life, given a book, a newspaper, TV news programme, or whatever, nobody comes along and sets us a series of specific tasks to foster understanding. We analyse the material and ask our own questions, just like students with a project. Life is a project, if you like to put it that way.

The next problem, if we want to persevere with project work, is how to teach students to do it well; in other words, how to introduce them to project work through easy project-type tasks that get progressively harder.

First, we can say that the early tasks will be small, i.e. involve few books and other materials and relatively little time.

Second, we will make it clear to students exactly what sort of analysis task is involved in doing a project, perhaps after this fashion:

Project – American Indians

When you do a project on a group of people like this, you always ought to find out these things:

(1)   How did they live?
(2)   What did they think?
(3)   What happened to them?

and you should break these big questions down like this:

How did they live? – What did they eat, what were their houses like, how big were the groups they lived in, how did they choose leaders?

What did they think? – What did they think about religion, what kind of things did they admire, what was their idea of a good man? What part in life did they think women should play?

What happened to them? – Are they still around, did they get conquered by somebody, did they change their way of life?

We get progression, as students get more familiar with project work, in two ways: increasing the number of main headings in the analysis, and reducing detailed guidance, or sub-headings. As in this example:

Project – Aztecs

Remember to think about six things when you do a project on a group of past people.

(1)   How did they live?
(2)   Why did they live like that?
(3)   What did they think?
(4)   How did their thought affect how they behaved?
(5)   What happened to them?
(6)   How do we know about them?

Remember under (1) to think about things like how they governed themselves, not just the food they ate and so on. Remember under (6) that we might have more than one sort of evidence about them.

In other words, we gradually make more complex demands, and give less guidance on how to meet those demands.

We are by no means out of the wood yet, because even if the students follow the given headings closely, they could still simply paraphrase books, and give purely descriptive accounts. So they need further guidance on analysis, of a similar kind to that we suggested you give them on note-taking (page 114). That involves you in giving them model examples and explaining those examples.

Exercise 8

Suppose we wanted to set up project work not on a group of people but on a celebrated individual, say Joan of Arc, or on an event, like a revolution or a war. Plan now (a) sets of 'easier' project instructions for those two cases, i.e. giving a few general headings and a lot of detailed guidance under those headings, and (b) sets of instructions for more advanced students, giving more general headings and less detailed guidance.

Exercise 9

Work out how, if at all, the suggested guidance on note-taking on pages 114-16 has to be amended or added to, in the case of advice on note-taking for project work.

Designating Materials to Use

With younger and less experienced students we will of course give much closer guidance on exactly what to read, and where to find it, than we would to older and more experienced ones.

There is no reason why a project should not be started off by students working through a set of small tasks designed by the teacher, of the type we are now familiar with. In our American Indian case, we could start with material, say, about Eastern Woodlands Indians, accompanied by a detailed question-sheet to work through, then put students on to Plains Indians material not accompanied by a work-sheet.

It goes without saying, of course, that when it comes to project work we cannot *assume* that any student, of any age, knows how to use an index or can make good use of a table of contents, can find his way round a library, knows that useful books might be found in library sections other than the history section, knows how to use a catalogue. Good students can do poor project work simply because they are unskilled in the mechanics of finding and using a book — let alone non-book materials.

We can do very useful small exercises in this area of what we might call 'library skills', e.g. setting students simply to note down the pages where references to Mussolini occur in a book on twentieth-century Europe; or at a later stage, simply noting where, in a library, there is material to be found on the Aztecs, apart from the 'History of Mexico' shelves.

Mixed Ability Groups and Project Work

Organisationally, project work fits well into a mixed-ability set-up. It involves individuals or small groupings working pretty much at their own pace, and it is very easy to set up student A to do a project with relatively little guidance, while less-able student B has the thing structured more carefully for him.

We could get into trouble, however, by encouraging student B to do a project which is inherently too difficult for his abilities. Sometimes it's obvious that a topic is too difficult, and we don't set it, or don't let a student choose it. Normally, for instance, a study of eschatological elements in later Hussite devotional writing would not recommend itself as a good field for fourteen-year-olds to try to plough. But it is less easy to decide whether a project, say, on the Ancient Greeks (granted there was plenty of material available) is harder than doing, say, the Aztecs.

Suppose we take our very simplest, three-part analysis of how to approach a project on a group of people in the past, i.e.

(1)   How did they live?

(2)　　What did they think?
(3)　　What happened to them?

We can see right away that doing the Greeks properly will involve
heavy emphasis on point 2, their ideas; heavy emphasis, in fact, on
some very difficult abstractions about science, democracy, and so on.
Point 2 will, of course, involve some difficult ideas in the case of the
Aztecs, but they at least might not be so central to the work as with
the Greeks.

What we have to do before letting a student embark on a topic is
work out ourselves what level of abstraction the student might get
involved with; decide how central the difficult ideas (which will come
up in any project whatsoever) are to the success of the whole; and then
judge whether a given student is likely to succeed at the project.

Just because a project might bring up some hard ideas, though, is
no reason for putting a student off it altogether. Suppose a student
wanted to do Ancient Greece. Suppose we guessed he could handle
the material culture side of things, and the 'what happened to them'
question, but would probably be thrown by the 'history of ideas'
element. It would be reprehensible of us to say 'miss out all that hard
stuff on ideas' — the best move would be to change the form of the
work at the relevant point.

We could arrange it like this. We could say, 'Find out about the
way the Greeks lived from Smith's book — just work on your own the
way I told you. When you are ready, go on to Jones's book on *The
Ideas of the Greeks* — that's a harder book, and there are some hard
ideas in it, so I want you to work through this question-sheet on
Jones's book — then you can go back to working on your own again,
for the rest of the project.'

A great deal of trouble can be headed off by anticipating in this
sort of way at least some of the potential sources of difficulty in a
project. Not so good is when the student says: 'Please, I'm getting
confused with this stuff about astronomy,' and a teacher has to figure
out a strategy for dealing with the problem on the spot. That will
happen sometimes anyway, but we can reduce these awkward
moments by good pre-planning.

A final point on the inherent difficulty of some projects. Students,
especially inexperienced and less able ones, will be more likely to
succeed in a project if the project involves similar kinds of operation
to those the student has been doing in recent class-work. For
example, some teachers commonly deal with a stretch of medieval

history in a straight political way – events, kings, battles and the like, and then go on to set up project work on 'The Monastery' or 'The Medieval Village'. Now, working on groups, like monks, involves asking different sorts of questions from the ones we ask about kings or battles. We could help students by not asking them to make this sudden switch; we could do class-work on monasteries, say, and then set up project work on 'The Village' – emphasising that a village is another sort of group, so the same kinds of questions will be appropriate for students to ask themselves about it as the teacher asked them about the monastery.

7. Synthesis

The skill of synthesis has a special importance in the context of school and of education generally. As adults, we might read a book on history or politics, making interpretations, evaluations and so on at a very high level, without having to articulate them, without having to put together or *synthesise* a series of evaluations and interpretations into connected written prose or oral exposition. For students, though, most of the time, it does not do them much good (in the eyes of their teachers, anyway) to have understanding, make good interpretations and so on, unless they can make an orderly and comprehensible synthesis in spoken or written form.

It is easy to see why skill or lack of skill in synthesis has come to loom so large in the way teachers assess students, and indeed in the way students assess themselves. Quite often the problems of synthesis are so pressing that the students' strengths and weaknesses in other skill-areas, and even the very existence of those other skills, are concealed from the teacher. The best way to approach the problems of synthesising as a skill might be through some examples of student writing. Let us compare these two pieces of student writing on the early days of the Indian Nationalist movement. (Assume that all the names and dates are correct.)

Student A

The first Indian Nationalist Congress was in 1886, the main leaders were Tilak and Gokhale. At first they were only interested in doing gymnastics and reading newspapers.

They were against the Muslims of India, who were not nationalists. The Muslims only felt nationalist about Turkey, not India, and were sad when Turkey was beaten in the war in 1912. This was

when the Italians attacked Libya to get a bigger Empire, to be more
equal to other countries with empires, i.e. England. The Indians
and Muslims fell out over Bengal in 1905 when the British divided
it up in a way that was better for Muslims.

Also in 1907, the Indians fell out within themselves and had to
split between the Tilak followers who wanted independence, right
away — and others who would just settle just for a Parliament in
India.

So the Indians had not just trouble with the British for freedom,
but with themselves and the Muslims.

Student B

The first Indian National Congress was in 1886. Indian nationalism
was affected by things *inside* India, and also *outside* things.

Outside was the Russo-Jap war in 1904 which helped National-
ism because it showed Asians could beat white soldiers. The
Muslims did not care about that so much as another thing, though
I suppose they would be fairly glad, but not so glad as the Hindus.
What the Muslims cared about more was in 1912 when Turkey
was attacked and England did not help Turkey. Turkey was a
Muslim country and, right from the start, the Muslims were not
happy about the Indian National Congress because of all the
Hindus in it; although the Muslims wanted freedom too. In 1905
the Hindus and Muslims and British fell out over dividing up
Bengal in a way to favour the Muslims. Also, around this time, the
Indian National Congress split up into two between Tilak and his
friends and others about how fast to try to get freedom or a
Parliament.

In 1914 India went to war against Germany, but, before this the
British undid the dividing of Bengal in 1911.

To start with student A. He obviously has, in his first paragraph,
failed to interpret properly something said by a book, or a teacher,
of the order 'The nationalists worked through gymnastic societies and
the press.' Paragraph two suggests a major failure successfully to
apply the idea of nationalism in the case of Indian Muslims, resulting
in a near-nonsense idea that they 'felt nationalistic about Turkey'.
(It would be interesting to try to work out exactly what information
about the Turco-Italian war had been misinterpreted here.) The
sentence beginning 'This war was when . . .' shows a wrong evaluation
of the relative importance of the details of the Turco-Italian war in

this context of the Indian nationalist movement. We must notice favourably, however, the orderliness of the exposition: paragraph one – foundation of INC; paragraph two – Hindu-Muslim dispute; paragraph three – INC internal strife; paragraph four – an excellent brief final summary of the whole matter. Student A has not done too badly at the skill called synthesis – the putting together of a series of understandings, information, judgements, etc., into a whole which is coherent, logical and clear.

We can see the importance of this skill if we look at the work of student B.

Student B starts off with an organising principle which sounds very useful – classification into 'things *inside* India and things *outside*'. Very soon, though, this leads him into a tortuous attempt to explain the Hindu-Muslim problem in the context of the Russo-Jap and Turco-Italian Wars. He fails, not surprisingly, to do this very lucidly. He then abandons this 'inside India, outside India' antithesis and uses very weak connecting ideas like 'Also around this time . . .' to connect the events. The conclusion is very lame. Notice how this lack of skill at synthesis, at putting it all together, obscures his much superior understanding, compared with student A, of nationalism, of the special problem of the Muslims, of the significance of the Turco-Italian war. His understanding of the split in the ranks of the INC sounds to be at least as good as that of student A, arguably better.

To some extent, as with the other skills, we can isolate the skill of synthesis, and take steps to improve students' expertise at it. Before we can go into that though, we must make an important point. Teachers often use synthesis, or rather, lack of skill at synthesis, as a sort of cognitive scapegoat. It is very obvious when students lack it, so people faced with students' writing that seems in some way unsatisfactory, are prone to say 'It lacks organisation', 'It does not hang together', and the like.

Students A and B both devote more space to the Turco-Italian war than seems appropriate. But student A does it, not because his organising, synthesising skill has faltered, but because of a serious lack of understanding about how the Muslims felt about Turkey. Student B seems to get in a tangle about Turkey genuinely because of a bad synthesising tactic – the attempt to introduce the Muslim problem for the first time in the unsatisfactory setting of two remote wars. So they both fall short of excellence – but for quite different reasons needing different remedial efforts.

As teachers, we will many, many times see student writing which strikes us as disordered, confused and badly put together. Always, we must ask, 'Is it confused like this because of lack of understanding of something – is it a failure deeper than just a lack of skill in synthesis?' Poor synthesis is like back pain – one easily identifiable symptom, but many different possible causes.

Exercise 10

Have a look at these two pieces on the question 'How could the English Parliament and Charles I have made peace in 1642 and prevented civil war?' They are both badly synthesised – but one of them might be a mess, partly because the student has misunderstood a fundamental concept, not simply because he lacks organisation. Which student is it, and what idea has he not understood?

Student A

There must be peace with France, because the King must stop all taxes and not ask Parliament for money, then Parliament would not mind him so much. He can get money from France and have to fight on their side. When that was over, France would have to let Parliament fight against the rebels in Ireland – OK, because they are Catholics and the King would not get money from Spain (Catholics). King must let Scots off and let them be Presbyterians (but not Catholics). Spain will be fought against in war by Parliament and King (because of the Catholics), but war against Scotland must be stopped because of Presbyterians.

Student B

Charles and Parliament will agree not to fight each other. They might get soldiers from Sweden or Switzerland to care for the country while they made peace. King Charles will agree to change religion of his, or let Scots have their own religion.

Both King Charles and Parliament must send soldiers home. But they must fight rebels in Ireland. King Charles I must try to makes taxes less and more fair somehow. They could have wars against Spain or Catholics in Germany and Ireland. They will agree on some place to meet and make a treaty.
['Answers' p.138]

Improving Synthesis

If somebody cannot reliably put together a coherent paragraph, it is not sensible to ask him to compose an essay of a thousand words. The first move we can make in improving the skill of synthesis is to think in terms of building up towards the long piece of consecutive prose, the essay, dissertation or whatever, by way of small written exercises which we make slowly longer and more complex as the student's skill grows. This has been heavily implied throughout this book so far – many of the suggested tasks for students have called for quite small pieces of writing.

Every task we can set, however small, so long as answering it involves writing more than about five words, also involves a synthesis task. The second basic move we can make to improve performance is to make explicit to students what we want of them, and discuss with them different ways material might be synthesised.

This last point is very important. Even in post-18 education, we meet students who are conscious of, and proud of, their ability to make their own interpretations and evaluations and so on, but accept the teacher as a complete authority on how to synthesise. So we get a teacher who says, 'Well, Mary, the content is good, but as a piece of prose the thing doesn't hang too well together – it doesn't really sock it across to me.' And Mary furrows her brow, and nods, just as if the teacher had said something that meant something to her.

Let us look at an example. Suppose we set a very simple translation task – maybe the very first one in the translation section. 'What is a rebellion?' We could work out in discussion in the class that there are five points to make, and write them on the board.

(1)   There have to be quite a lot of people in it.
(2)   The people involved are not just bandits.
(3)   The people fight.
(4)   They have some kind of cause, or plan, or grievance.
(5)   They fight against a government which is in some sense established.

We then ask, 'What is the best order to make these points in?' There are, in fact, several different orders that make perfectly good sense. Students must learn that there is not usually one 'logical' way to synthesise things; they must practise devising their own 'logics'. They must then practise giving reasons for the way they have arranged the points as they would give reasons for, say, an evaluation or an interpretation.

We could then ask, 'Could we present the answer a different way maybe through an invented example, what about if we said, "If there was a rebellion in Barataria, the following three things would happen." Try doing it that way and see if you like it better or not.' With even this very small piece of writing, involving less than a hundred words, there is scope to discuss different *forms* of presentation, as well as different *orders* of presenting points.

There are, in fact, few cases where there is one obviously superior way to synthesise material. Even where straight chronological narrative is involved, this is so. Suppose we set a complex task involving a good deal of writing: 'Why did Australia never rebel against England like America did?' Even if we gave students a great deal of guidance on the lines of 'Remember you will need to use the terms "nationalism, "tariff" and "imperialism"; you will need to be careful on the differences between "economic" points and "political" points,' and so on, there is still scope for choice about how to do the synthesis job. Two obvious ways to present the end product are the chronological, going through potential '1776' moments of Australian history and saying why in fact separatism did not flourish; or setting up some general thesis and illustrating it with incidents not necessarily in chronological order. Or perhaps the whole thing could be done in the form of an imaginary dialogue.

So nearly always, we can sensibly ask, as part of the task-setting routine – 'How do you plan to present the answer?' or, as part of the feedback routine, 'Why did you present the answer like this?'

Although we want students to be highly conscious of taking their own decisions about the synthesising process, it is also a very suitable area in which to present them with models.

The best synthesiser in the room is probably you, by a long way, so let the students see you in action sometimes. Build up different plans for 'answers' and essays, on the board, explaining your decisions as you go along.

Exercise 11

Choose a set of tasks, either out of this book or of your own devising, and practise two things:

(a) Thinking out how many different ways an answer could be put together or 'synthesised' (remembering both the questions of different *ordering* of material and different *forms* of answer).

(b) Plan how you would show and explain to a class some of the different ways of presenting the 'answer' in each case.

Problems with Literacy

It may be that a student's ability to construct even a coherent sentence is very poor; or that his spelling is so bad that you really can't always make sense of what he writes. In such cases our general pattern of working through small, specific-task exercises, where he can use oral responses and a small amount of writing, is better than many strategies: certainly better than the common pattern of extensive teacher-talk; note-copying; 'now write about it.' But the skill of synthesis seems to be about end products, and very largely about written ones — so we must be able to improve the skill of synthesis of someone who cannot even write properly.

There are two basic synthesis exercises: deciding on and justifying the order in which to present material, and similarly deciding on and justifying the form of presentation. The first thing we can get poor writers to do, is do the synthesis exercise, like our example of 'rebellion', without actually having to write down the final version. In other words, we skip round their inability to synthesise *written* language at sentence or phrase level, and go straight on to higher-level problems. This could be pretty important to improving their motivation: you could, in school, meet students who have never successfully tackled a synthesis problem involving more than one paragraph, simply and only because they have never, ever, got past composing the first paragraph of any piece of history writing before the bell went.

Another way to tackle the problem of ordering material, without being involved in extensive writing, is to get students to order pictures, maps, graphs, and so on, which are either self-explanatory, or better still, require some short caption. The important thing here is that there is a genuine ordering challenge — for example: with the Trafalgar campaign of 1805, we could make a simple block graph of the relative strength of the two fleets, a diagram of Nelson 'breaking the line' of the Franco-Spanish fleet, a picture of Nelson's death, sketch maps of Napoleon's 1804 invasion plan, a picture of a warship of the time — in other words, material which can genuinely be ordered and presented in different ways, to tell a story.

Most of the materials in this Trafalgar example could have been produced by the students in earlier sessions — this is the kind of economy in use of resources to aim for; you may start off full of picture-gathering zeal in September, but by December you could be running out of both zeal and materials, so the trick is to use simple materials, student-made or home-made and re-use them for different purposes, wherever you can.

Giving Feedback

The two precious things you offer students with writing problems are these: occasions on which they need to compose their own prose, in order to do tasks which they find interesting; and, second, success at composing prose. Both could be greatly undermined if we do not mark their work skilfully.

If we under-mark, as it were, and simply praise work which they know to be badly spelled and ill-constructed, they will rapidly suspect that they are being patronised. If we red-ink every spelling error and every awkwardness of syntax, they could easily be discouraged. What we need is a consistent and reasonable policy on spelling and syntax mistakes.

A reasonable policy — on spelling mistakes — might be this: *never* ignore all of them, and never red-ink more than three on one piece of work. Pick on mistakes in spelling important, common words — 'because', 'battle', 'reason'; rather than 'revenue', 'guerrilla' or 'entente'. With syntax or grammar errors, again, take note of not more than two per piece of work — or less if the piece is brief. Never simply indicate that a phrase or sentence is wrong — say what is wrong and write in a correct version. There is nothing more irritating for a student than an indication that a mistake has been made, with no clue as to what that mistake might be.

The policy outlined above for spelling mistakes and grammar or syntax errors could be applied when we comment on any student's work, whether he has a major writing problem or not.

But there is far more to commenting on work than that. The reason why we comment on work at all is presumably to encourage students and to try to improve the next piece of work by pointing out the strength and weaknesses of the piece of work before us.

Certain principles of commenting follow from this. In most circumstances, a comment should contain praise. There are cases where praise would be inappropriate, but they are far fewer than the cases in which praise might be given and is not. Teachers sometimes seem extremely reluctant to praise, which is a pity, since praise is the easiest of motivational devices to use, and a very powerful one.

Give the praise *first*. It will have more effect that way, and you are less likely to forget to give it at all, if your first move in planning a comment on students' work is always, 'What can I say here that is good?'

When you have singled out a passage or phrase or word for praise, say what it is you like about it, as precisely as you can. If, say, a student has illustrated a general statement with an example of their own, praise that tactic specifically and they will be much more likely to do it again.

The need to be specific is even greater when you single out something for criticism. A great deal of what teachers write on students' work is not even read by students — possibly because it conveys no clear message. Avoid putting things like question marks and exclamation marks in the margin. Don't just underline passages; don't be sarcastic.

As well as being specific, be constructive. Say clearly how the student might do better next time. Saying 'Try to be more relevant; think for yourself more' helps nobody.

If there are many things to criticise, do not pick them all out. Use the same rule suggested for spelling errors and only pick out two or three main points. A lot of red ink on one's work is a depressing sight, however useful and constructive the remarks are.

Here is an example of how a piece of work might be marked on these principles.

Student A

Total War in World War II

(1)   To an extent unequalled even by the massive conflict of a quarter century earlier, World War II was a 'total' war.

(2)   The most dreadful thing in the whole of the war's time was the killing of all the Jews in German concentration camps. The bombing of many German cities such as Dresden and Hamburg was also a crime against Humanity, but the killing of the jews came first.

(3)   The next worst thing was all the refugees who lost their homes and had to travel to camps where some of them still were many years after the war.

(4)   I think the next worst thing was Stalingrad because so many people were killed and the soldiers had to fight in the cold, so cold that when they were wounded their blood froze to the ground where they were. And, equally bad also, was Leningrad where everybody in this whole city was starved.

(5)   Fathers and brothers having to go away for years and years and may be killed, was the worst thing for ordinary people.

(6)   Rationing, mobilisation of industry and manpower, social change, further change in the roll of women were also terrible parts of this truly terrible war.

(The paragraphs are numbered only for ease of reference — normally, of course, remarks would be written nearer to the text commented on.)

Remarks on Student A's Work: A good answer on what you think were the worst things in the war — each point clearly made, separate from other points.

Next time — (a) always put things in your own words, don't *copy* like in paragraph (1) and (6). (b) When there is a new word to use, like 'total' war, tell me somewhere what you think it means, maybe at the end. On this task you might have said — 'To sum up, "total war" is when . . .'

Exercise 12

Write remarks on these following examples of students' work.

Student B

Total War in World War II

To an extent unequalled even by the massive conflict of a quarter-century earlier, World War II was a 'total' war.

To prove this the first fact is that World War II had battles in many more places than before, in Burma and Africa and China and also a lot more bombing of towns by aircraft and more U-boats sinking ships. In 1914-18 nearly all the battles were in Europe, except for the campaign in East Africa where a most gallant force of German troops and native 'Askaris' held off greatly superior forces of British and Indian troops for the duration of the war.

Many of the battles in 1914-18 war, were very bloody, much worse than World War II, e.g. The Somme, Paschendale. But World War II was a total war because everybody had to be in the army and in 1914 it was volonteers.

The worst thing in the war was the concentration camps in Germany where millions of Jews were killed with gas. There were also great bombings of German towns, i.e. Dresden but these were not as bad as the concentration camps were, because the Germans started the war, and using gas is worse even than bombing people.

Back in England, the thing most people remember is rationing, about the war. Even children's sweets were rationed which showed how this was truly a 'total war'.

Student C

Nationalism in 1914

Serbia is a small country fighting for Nationalism. In my opinion, Serbia was the course of World War I. Serbia was full of many nationalist fanatics. Serbia started trouble which made Austria declare war on Serbia. Serbia had an ally — Russia!! Austria was scared of Russia so Austria got Germany to help them out.

So France and England next joined Russia to fight Austria, Germany and Italy.

I do not think Austria is much to fault for causing World War I. They had to fight against Serbia.

Student D

Nationalism in 1914

In my opinion it was Austria most to blame. If they had not wanted to get Serbia more of it would have happened and they only want Serbia for themselves not for Serbians' good. Russia disagreed so all countries started to fight.

France, Italy and Germany were not much to blame, they only helped other countries like Serbia and Austria who had themselves to blame. Russia and France and England fought four years three months against Germany and Austria who lost.

Student A

Sutton Hoo

I am a Viking warrior in a viking village near Sutton Hoo. The King and hos warrior's were going on a hunt and I had to guard the village. The village was all made out of wood and thier were about twenty huts in the village. The village was surrounded by a wall of logs to protect it. The village was quite lively with children playing people talking. There were cows and chickens in the village. When the hunting party came back the king was luying over his horse dead, they took him in his hut. I went to one of the warrior's and he told me that they were chasing a boar and another one went in front of the kings horse and the horse bucked and the king fell off and broke his neck. When the warriors told the village a week of moaning started everybody was sad and praying and crying. After the week passed we started digging a borrow. When the hole was dug we took a ship and dragged it under rollers. When they got it in the hole they put the king's body in the ship then they put all his treasures with him. Then they started dancing and praying. They put all his treasures with him so he will be weathy in the other world. Then they covered the hole up. Then the council made me the king.

Student E

Sutton Hoo

One day in a village a king died and the next day the Saxons had a mourning. It lasted a whole week and then they started to dig a hole and they put a ship into the hole and then they put in his treasures into the ship. The king got killed by a battle and he got shot by anarow. The kings name was called Englebert. Then they put the king in the bout and they dug a tunnel and put a boulder in front of the tunnel. Then they shosed a new king.

Student G

Sutton Hoo

In a Village near Sutton Hoo the king had just died and all the people are in mourning and know one knows how he died but they think he's been posiand they are just diging the burial hole. The king was king Edward his town was not very big with wooden hits dotted about. They have just finished diging the burial hole. Here comes the ship being dragged to the hole before they put the ship in they put all his treasure in to the ship then they put the body in to the ship and put ship in the hole. Then they start to dance up and down. After they have finished dancing they put the rock in front of the cave.

Student H

Sutton Hoo

The village was a collection of wooden huts and wooden fense which was now brocen down. Their had been an attack on our saxon village. But the most disterbing thing was the kingsdeath. King edmund had bean killed in repeling the invaders. the howel village was in mourning for seven days. Then the peopledug the burial hole. We draged the ship up to the hole we put the ship in to the hole (without the mast or sails) and plased all the treasures of the deak

king in to the boat we then plased the body in andheld a servise.
The people sadly make a Barrow and closed it up. The barrow was
so high on the hill that you could sea it for miles and remember
his grateness.

Project Work and Synthesis

In the above examples, it may have struck you that the students might
have done better work if they had been set a more clearly defined task.
The students may have been carefully briefed on how to answer on
'Total War in World War II' but as it stands it is an indefinite sort of
title, leaving unclear exactly what the teacher wants the student to do.
As we have observed before, the first essential step to getting good
student work is to set a good, clear task.

With project work, by definition, though, the students to some
extent have to set their own tasks. This gives an extra dimension to the
synthesis problem with project work and the analysis section has
something to say about this. Project work, though, offers a useful
opportunity in the field of synthesis, as well as an extra difficulty.
It offers the chance to students to make genuine, major decisions
about the form of presentation, as well as its ordering. In their
earliest, preparatory project work, students should be set problems
like: 'Would words or a map or a graph make this point best? Could we
have an imaginary dialogue to get this point across? Which of these
pictures illustrate the subject best – or would a picture plus a map
be better?'

As well as encouraging them to think out different ways of synthesising material, and encouraging them not to assume that words is the
only way, we must give them practice in criticising ways of presentation.
Thus, if a student includes, say, a picture in a project, he must be asked
questions like 'What is it for? Is it just decoration or is it illustrating
something? Would this other picture be better for your purpose?'

Putting together your end product in a way which you can explain
and justify is as important a part of the whole process of tackling a
task as any other part. When students both understand and agree with
that proposition they have taken the major step towards excellence in
the skill of synthesis.

Exercise 10 – Suggested Answers

Student B's idea of Swedish troops acting as a kind of UN force in
1642 England is eccentric, but much more serious is student A's lack
of understanding of the idea of taxes ('King must stop all taxes . . .

He can get money from France'). The misguided ingenuity of the idea of the government being run on money from France then leads to the confusions of the first half of the piece. It also lets student A lose sight completely of the need to elaborate some kind of deal between King and Parliament, in his welter of complicated wars.

Neither A nor B have put together particularly well-ordered, well-synthesised answers, but student A's apparent lack of grasp of the idea of taxation is what needs tackling first.

Synthesis – Generalising

Suppose a student had considered and listed these facts about the world in 1945:

(1)   World War II was over.
(2)   Many soldiers and concentration camp prisoners were able to go home.
(3)   Many factories turned back to peacetime work.
(4)   People were scared by the A-bomb.
(5)   Trouble was beginning between Russia and the West.
(6)   Many people in Europe were refugees with nowhere to go.
(7)   New wars were on the boil in Indonesia, China, Vietnam.
(8)   Britain and other European countries were much poorer than in 1939.

Suppose we then said to the student, 'Make the shortest accurate general statement you can about the way things stood in 1945, basing your statement on that list.' We have asked the student to generalise. Generalising is a kind of synthesis, of 'putting together', but it involves more than putting together a good piece of prose, so it is worth thinking about separately. We can see what it involves by looking at some answers to that particular 1945 task we just set.

Student A: 'Europe in 1945 was in a mess.'
Student B: 'Wars settle nothing.'
Student C: 'The war was over but there was trouble with Russia and many refugees. Also war in China and Vietnam. The Atom bomb scared people.'

Student A's answer clearly falls short of being a good generalisation because it takes account of only part of the facts and ignores Asia. Student B goes far beyond the given facts, and comes up with the historian's bugbear — 'a wild generalisation'. Student C has not got a generalisation at all. He has done what students very often do, when asked to generalise, or 'summarise', or 'pull it all together' — he has taken it to mean 'condense', and pulled out a few of what he takes to be the salient elements in the material. He has not done the central act involved in generalising, i.e. come up with a new concept or concepts to apply to the facts.

'New concept' does not have to be as high-flown as it sounds. In this context, some quite ordinary ideas, but ideas which are not present in the original list, will serve, e.g. 'good things' and 'problems', giving, for instance, the generalisation 'In 1945, some good things were happening, but there were also many problems.' Student A offered 'mess' as his 'new concept' and it is a genuine example, if a bit crude.

To sum up — a good generalisation actually is a generalisation — it offers some general concept, thought up by the student, and applied to the given set of information. This general concept can be quite simple — like 'mess' or 'good thing' or 'problem'. It takes account of all the given information, but does not (like student B) go beyond the information.

We ought to consider two points before we get down to business on how to improve students' skill in generalising. First, a 'good' generalisation does not have to be one the teacher agrees with. When a student asks himself, 'What simple, general term or idea best expresses what I want to say about this set of facts?' there is clearly a large evaluation element in that question. Suppose a student, when asked to generalise on those given facts about 1945 said, 'The end of World War II meant the world got instantly duller, but there were hopeful signs of some excitement for the future, notably the A-bomb.' We might not like what he says, but by the three criteria we have offered, we cannot say that it is bad generalisation.

Second, the very term generalisation is often viewed by teachers, especially history teachers, with suspicion. Should we be teaching it at all? Should we not rather be teaching students *not* to generalise, but to avoid generalisation, to have a scholarly emphasis on the particular truth of particular instances?

It is probably student B's type of ill-founded and sweeping generalisation which has brought the whole process into ill-repute with history teachers. This is a pity, because generalising is not so much a desirable skill as an unavoidable one, if we are to have discourse at all with each other. 'Abraham Lincoln had many problems' is a simple generalisation. If we cannot speak and write at that level of generality, we can hardly communicate at all. However, as we shall see, promoting good generalising does not involve being easy on sloppy, wild or other-wise unscholarly utterances.

Improving the Skill of Generalising

As with the other skills, the keys to success are: start early, with the youngest students; make clear what you want; give examples; give lots of small-scale practice.

The earliest sorts of exercises might involve application exercises, where we give the students the possible generalising concepts, or 'summing up' words, and ask them if they think they apply. For instance, 'We have to write just one sentence to sum up what we have learned about the early days of the New England colonies, would it be best to say, "The colonists had many *battles*, or many *difficulties,* or had the *worst* time anyone ever had"?'

In such a very simple way we can make the points that a summary should be brief, and hinge around one or two 'new words', that it should not go beyond the fact ('*worst time* anyone ever had') nor fail to take account of all the facts (*battle*).

At the earliest stage, we should also introduce the idea of tentative-ness, of 'maybe', 'up to a point' and 'perhaps'. Our parallel use of tasks of evaluation, tasks on interpreting sources, and 'what might have happened' extrapolation games should all be strengthening their grasp of the concept that history is not a series of teacher-stated truths. However, we can also reinforce the concept, and teach the language of tentativeness directly, quite early and simple, as here: 'Now let's sum up about the Pilgrim Fathers' first year in America — which would it be better to say, "They had shown that colonies *would succeed* in America", or should we say that "Colonies *might perhaps succeed*"?'

The next, critical, stage is for students to make up their own generalisation unaided. At first, they could have the information to be generalised about in a handy form, like a list, made up either by you or by them, like the '1945' list at the start of this section.

A useful task for a further stage would be to give students generalisations about material at the start of a topic, and make the theme of the work on that topic the checking out of how true the original generalisation was. Thus, work on the Communist world might check out a generalisation like 'Communism only gained power in backward countries.' Learning about Czechoslovakia and East Germany, as well as Russia and China, could lead the students to make a better generalisation of their own, knowing from the start of the work that

that was what they were ultimately trying to do.

As with some other skills, especially synthesis, 'Knowing that that is what they were ultimately trying to do' is the key to success with generalising — that is, awareness of it by students as a separate skill; a knowledge of precisely what criteria of excellence are being applied by the teacher; confidence from the knowledge of having done it many times before.

Exercise 13

Make up lists of eight or more items, on historical material of your choice, about which you could ask students to write a simple, one-sentence generalisation.

3 METHODS IN ACTION

In this chapter we deal with two matters that have not been touched on at all, except very lightly; the use of books, and history field-work. These are activities which offer such special problems, and which are so central in a history teacher's work, that they deserve separate treatment, for the sake of clarity. Also in Chapter 3 we deal at some length with the question of putting together our various techniques and types of tasks and questions into the sort of fairly lengthy teaching sequences in which teachers actually try to organise their work.

First, though, we turn to a matter which has been referred to more than once already, but which is of such basic importance that it must, now, have a separate and more leisurely treatment — the question of students' differing abilities.

1. Planning for Mixed-Ability Groups

Throughout the sections on the various intellectual skills, we have mentioned the problem of allowing for students' greater or lesser abilities. Most explicitly, in the section on translation and interpretation we suggested three rules of thumb for setting tasks at an easier level without abandoning the learning-goal: shorten the task; simplify the language in which the task is set; break the task into its component parts. In the section on application we added to the simple idea of 'shortening' the idea of reducing the number of factors of which the student is required to take note in historical problems.

We need to have a separate review and pull-together of this question of abilities, though, away from the context of any specific skill, for two reasons. First, the fundamental importance of this question in a teacher's work: virtually any class of students, anywhere, can fairly be described as a 'mixed-ability group', whether they are allegedly 'streamed' or not. In any case, we may well sometimes be teaching the same historical material with two or more different age-groups. So no teacher can avoid this question. Second, at the moment of writing, there is a noticeable shortage, in the history-social studies area, of answers to this plain question: 'What makes a task harder or easier than another task?' Defeatist approaches to the question, of the order 'let the less able ones draw pictures' are still being publicly propounded.

First, let us consider what we mean when we say John is 'less able than Debby'. Suppose someone set John and Debby the same task – how might their response differ? Take the case of the task 'Account for Hitler's rise to power in Germany.' If John is 'less able' we might expect him, compared with Debby to:

(1)   *Write less.*

(2)   *Write less well* from the angle of grammar, spelling, syntax, and so on.

(3)   *Write less relevantly* – he might put something like 'Adolph Hitler was born in 1889; first he was an artist in Vienna, being born in Austria, and then a soldier in World War I. He got the Iron Cross.' He might write this way for one of two main reasons – he may not understand the task, and so may actually think his response appropriate. Or he may just be so slow and incompetent at writing that what was meant as a preamble turns out to be the whole 'answer'.

(4)   *Give some factors which are relevant undue prominence* – for example, 'There was great fear of Communism widespread, mass unemployed set in about 1930; people were afraid. Afraid of Russia, and revolution and all thought the Treaty of Versailles was unfair. Also Hitler's party of the NSDAP was well ruled and organised with propaganda, played up for fear of the "Reds".' Here again, the response gives (arguably) too much space to the Communist threat because John is inept at the skill of synthesis, or possibly because he does not understand that Russia, 'the Reds', and revolution, and Communism, are virtually the same thing said in different ways. Or maybe he just writes slowly: if the response was twice as long (and the rest of it did not mention Communism) the thing would look less badly balanced.

(5)   *Stick in passages from books verbatim* – i.e. without trying to translate or interpret them.

(6)   *Give wrong interpretations of books or of the teacher's statements.* Sometimes teachers call this, confusingly, 'getting the facts wrong'. Suppose John put the following, though: 'All the other parties like Centre and Social Democrats were in favour of Hitler so, he got in easily.' The most plausible explanation for this error is misinterpretation by John of some teacher – or book-phrase like 'Centre and S.D. parties played into Hitler's hands by . . . and so inadvertently helped him.' It is not the same kind of error as saying, 'Hitler became Chancellor in 1931', a factual-recall error about a date, and it is much better to think of it as a failure of interpretation than to confuse it

with such factual-recall errors.

(7) *Show unmistakable signs of not grasping concepts.* Suppose John puts 'The first thing Hitler did in 1933 was set himself up with camps for enemies as a Dictator. And plans for war on the world. The first country he attacked was the Rhineland from France. Then Czechoslovakia and Austria.' He has plainly not understood the idea 'rise to power in Germany' and his lack of understanding is not, this time, obscured by his slowness in writing or lack of synthesis skill.

We could obviously take this analysis further, but we have said enough to show this: when we say 'John has given a less good answer than Debby', it could mean any or all of at least seven things, ranging from merely a less complete answer by John to an answer by John showing various fundamental misunderstandings. Another thing is also clear – that in several of the examples of John's responses, it is not easy to tell exactly what has gone wrong – lack of actual writing skill and speed, or lack of understanding, or what.

So we need a policy for setting John an easier version of this task which will do three things. First, keep him to the same basic learning task as Debby: 'Draw a picture of a swastika-flag' is not the sort of task that will help John to improve. Second, make it easier for him to write a good response. Third, if he cannot write a good response, at least make it clearer to the teacher exactly where he is going wrong.

Let us start with the original task: 'Account for Hitler's rise to power.' If we apply to it our basic three-part technique: 'Size of task; language of task; break task into parts' – we might get something of this sort – 'Make a list of four main things that helped Hitler to rise to power: think of the way things were in Germany, and also of the things that Hitler did to help himself.'

Let us work through the seven-point list of John's deficiencies again, and see if this revised task will meet the three criteria we have set ourselves.

Points 1 and 2 – volume, grammar, syntax, etc. Asking for a list should certainly put less strain on John's writing powers than the mini-essay of the original task.

Point 3 – the list-format lets John off the need for a preamble, so he will not waste time on irrelevancies like Hitler's date of birth, etc. If he does, at least we know for sure he does not understand what to do.

Point 4 – undue prominence to certain factors. If John really is not seeing that 'Reds' = Russia = Communism, this new task will not help him to be more successful than he was with the old one. It will, though, make his error easier to spot with certainty.

Point 5 — verbatim quotations from books. The new task makes it quite difficult for John to make the 'verbatim quote' response at all. He is virtually driven to use his own words, and so be more successful in this respect at least.

Point 6 — wrong interpretation of books or teacher's words. As with *Point 7* — failure to grasp concepts — the element of 'clue-giving' in the new task (think of the way things were in Germany: think of what Hitler did to help himself) might help a little bit to point John the right way. Basically, though, the new task probably just makes the misunderstanding clearer to the teacher.

To sum up: the new task will make it a great deal easier for the teacher to make out what is going on in John's mind. In so far as it simplifies the organisation of the end product it helps John to give a better answer, by letting him concentrate on essentials. It is, in other words, a genuinely 'easier' task of real usefulness to John and his teacher — provided John has understood the central concept, 'rise to power'.

If he has failed to grasp the main concept, what can we do?

Well, one thing we can do is not get in this fix in the first place, that is, not set tasks involving difficult ideas like 'rise to power' before making sure the students have grasped them, through short exercises involving translation, extrapolation, etc.

But that is pretty unhelpful of course. Nobody can head off every possible difficult idea that way and however well we teach consciously for concept development we are going to find ourselves needing to know how to present a concept in an easier form because some students cannot handle it in the form we first thought of it. 'Easier form' in this context means 'nearer to the concrete'. In the case of 'rise to power' that means going down to, say, 'persuades people to let him be leader'.

It is very important to be able to do quickly and easily this sort of transformation 'Hitler's rise to power' — 'Hitler persuading people to let him be leader'. It is at the centre of the teacher's art of simplification and, in class, you might have to do it at any moment, orally, when a student asks you for an explanation of an abstraction. The key is that the 'easier' form has concrete nouns in it ('people', 'leader') and, as it were, 'concrete verbs' — like 'persuade', verbs where you can form a mental picture of somebody doing whatever it is. You can't so readily form a mental picture of somebody 'rising'.

Here is a fairly full example, showing how sometimes you can even take abstractions 'down to the concrete' in more than one stage. The key difficult abstractions are emphasised with italics.

Version 1: 'How might, *environmental* changes *affect* the *material culture* of a *primitive community*?'

Version 2: 'How might, say, changes in the climate change the way of life of, for instance, a Stone Age tribe?'

Version 3: We can still get nearer the concrete with the terms 'climate' and 'way of life' thus: 'Suppose the weather got a lot colder, and stayed cold all the time. With a Stone Age tribe, how might that change (a) the clothes they wore, (b) their houses or shelters, (c) food they ate?' (See how the ideas of 'nearer the concrete' and 'breaking the task down' coincide here.)

We could suppose a version 4, where we make the idea 'Stone Age' even more concrete with a picture and said 'look at the people in the picture . . . suppose where they lived it got a lot colder . . .' etc.

If, of course, students still couldn't give an answer at version 3 or 4, we could presume they didn't understand the whole idea of environment influencing material culture and we would have to introduce it from scratch.

Exercise 1

Here are two tasks. In each case, write an easier version by bringing the abstract ideas involved nearer to the concrete — if you can, make your easier version easier yet. (Both tasks are phrased at a pretty elevated level at the start, to make your task easier.)

(1)   What was the impact of the abolition of slavery in 1833 on British-Caribbean society?

(2)   What were the economic and political issues in the dispute between Britain and her American colonies?

Summary and Further Example

One way to approach the question of differing abilities is to plan to set different students different tasks according to their abilities. If we do this, an easier task should:

(a)   be addressed to the same basic learning as the harder tasks;

(b)   be shorter, use easier task-setting language, be broken down into its component parts where appropriate, have fewer factors for students to consider; and

(c)   the language in which difficult ideas are expressed should be nearer to the concrete than in harder tasks.

To reinforce the idea of tackling the learning of the same concept in ways suitable to students of different abilities, we should now practise stringing together series of tasks on the same concept, each task at two levels. Here is an example. In the example, the different skills are employed in the same order in which we set them in this book – in real life, of course, there is no reason to have students practise skills in that particular order.

Concept: 'Underdeveloped' (as in 'Underdeveloped Countries')

Translation Task

Version 1: Say in your own words what you think 'under-developed' means.

Version 2: Say how the people in an underdeveloped country might live differently from how we do: think about food, schools, sorts of work they do, houses.

Interpretation Task

Version 1: Read this passage and say why the writer thinks Spain is a 'peculiarly interesting' case of an underdeveloped country.

Version 2: Read this passage and say: (a) why did people think Spain was rich in the sixteenth/seventeenth centuries; and (b) why the writer thinks Spain should really have been seen as an 'under-developed' country.

The Passage

Spain in the sixteenth and seventeenth centuries was a peculiarly interesting case of a poor, or as we might say nowadays, 'under-developed' country.

Because of the huge masses of gold and silver which Spain got from South America and Mexico, she was able to pay great armies of soldiers, and conduct great wars for over a hundred years. She fought the English, the French, the Turks, the Dutch, the Venetians – and won many great victories between 1520 and 1640. She was able to act militarily exactly like a very rich country.

But all the time, the silver was going straight from Cadiz to the Spanish armies. Hardly anyone in Spain got their hands on any of it.

Spaniards were living in poverty. Spain had a bad soil, some bad farming methods, a harsh climate, not many industries. Useful minerals like iron were not dug out as much as they could have been. So most Spaniards lived in poverty, in a poor country.

Meantime, foreigners looked at Spain's silver, and great armies and said, 'What a great and rich nation is Spain!'

Application Tasks

Version 1: Here are some facts about Sylvania: is Sylvania an 'underdeveloped' country?

(1)   About 100 Sylvanians are millionaires (in dollars).
(2)   The population is pretty large — 80 million.
(3)   There is still plenty of spare room in the country.
(4)   The capital city is impressive — many skyscrapers.
(5)   Most Sylvanians leave school at 12.
(6)   Most Sylvanians are farmers.
(7)   Average farm size is 6 acres.
(8)   There are big oil deposits, just starting to be drilled.

Version 2: Here are some facts about Sylvania: is Sylvania an 'underdeveloped' country?

(1)   About 100 Sylvanians are millionaires (in dollars).
(2)   Most Sylvanians are farmers.
(3)   Most Sylvanians farms are about 6 acres.
(4)   Most Sylvanians leave school at 12.
(5)   The population is large — 80 million.

Extrapolation Tasks

Version 1: Suppose around about 1940, a citizen of one of the underdeveloped countries had made a great revolutionary industrial invention. Sketch in the possible sequence of events — would that country have ceased to be underdeveloped, or what?

Version 2: Suppose round about 1940, a citizen of one of the underdeveloped countries we have been learning about (say Mexico) had invented the jet engine. What would have happened next? Would the inventor have tried to sell his invention in Mexico, or somewhere else, do you think? Would the factories to build the engine be in Mexico or somewhere else? Would Mexico get to be a rich country because of this invention by one of her people?

Evaluation Tasks

Version 1: If an underdeveloped country could direct big extra resources to just one of the following, which should it be?

Technical education — health services — general education — prospecting for minerals — subsidies to farmers — industrial investment?

Version 2: Suppose you were the government of an under-developed country like Mexico and you had a lot of money from somewhere which you could only spend on *one* thing from this list. Which ought you to choose, and why?

Schools — money to farmers — building factories — people to go round showing new methods to farmers?

Analysis Task

Version 1: Read the section on Zaire in Jones' book, pages 57-65. Make notes to compare and contrast Zaire and Mexico as underdeveloped countries.

Version 2: Read Jones, pages 59-62. Put the first sentence into your own words. Make a list of three main ways in which Zaire is like Mexico as an underdeveloped country.

Synthesis Task

Version 1: Write a handbook of advice — about 1,000 words — to somebody setting out to help 'underdeveloped countries'.

Version 2: Write a list of five or six main problems you think an underdeveloped country has. Then write a paragraph saying how you might try to solve any two of them.

Exercise 2

Try to put together strings of pairs of tasks like this, using a concept of your choice as the focus. Try putting the use of the various skills in different orders from the order we have used, to see how it turns out.

Exercise 1 — Levels of Difficulty — Answers

(1)   'Impact', 'abilition', 'British-Caribbean-Society' are the obvious candidates for 'taking down to the concrete'. (Slavery certainly is an abstraction, but if that term is not understood, the usefulness of the whole task would be doubtful.) Version 2 might be — 'What was the effect of doing away with slavery in 1833 on the people who lived in

the Caribbean islands that belong to Britain?'

'Effect' in turn might be expressed in a Version 3 in this way: 'After they did away with slavery in 1833, what happened to the people who lived . . .' etc. Outside the terms of the present exercise, of course, we would *reduce* the task by asking only about, say, Jamaica; and *break down* 'people' into ex-slaves, ex-owners, and so on.

(2)   'Economic', 'political', 'issues', 'dispute', 'Britain' and 'American colonies' are the terms to 'take down'.

Version 2, perhaps — 'In the quarrel between the Government in Britain and the people in the American colonies, how exactly did they disagree about (a) money and taxes and (b) questions of government?'

Version 3, more concrete yet, might perhaps involve making that final phrase 'questions of government' into 'what laws to have, and who should make them'.

2. Using Books

We have referred in several contexts to students making use of books, most especially in the context of the skill of analysis. Books are so important in a teacher's work, and problems about books loom so large sometimes, that the question of history books deserves at least a small section to itself.

Teachers have two main problems about books — selecting them, in the first place, and, second, using books which they didn't select, don't like much, but have to use because they are the only ones available.

Selecting Books

Books must clearly be scholarly and accurate: but there are other principles of selection.

Before we can have principles on which to select books, we have to have an idea of what we think books are for. So far, in the sections on the various skills, we have assumed a certain function for books in the general scheme of history teaching, but we ought to make that assumption explicit now.

We assume that books are things which teachers ought to use to set specific tasks using the full range of cognitive skills, in order to foster concept development. Books are not repositories of information into which students can dip and ladle out information when they or the teacher thinks it appropriate.

Task A:

Read and make notes on the following passage:

One of the greatest signs of the new spirit of the Renaissance was a growing awareness of the workings of the universe. With the disappearance of the medieval fear that too deep an enquiry into Nature would upset the balance between God and man, there were rapid advances in scientific knowledge.

During the fifteenth century Leonardo da Vinci was the leading scientist of the age. Da Vinci was a man of very wide interests, who was always too busy to put his ideas into actual use. Despite this, he was in every way a scientist, using observation and research to overcome any problem with which he was faced. In order to paint and draw more naturally da Vinci made a careful study of anatomy, dissecting corpses and carefully drawing the actions of muscles and limbs. Having a very active mind he was very interested in the behaviour of animals and birds, and took especial note of winged flight. This led him to study the problems of manned flight, and he drew up the first known plans for a helicopter. In the same way da Vinci designed a paddle steamer. The great weakness of these plans was that there was no power to drive these machines, and for this reason his designs were lost and forgotten for several centuries.

Da Vinci was several centuries ahead of the contemporaries in many other respects. He advanced the theory that light travelled in waves, and experimented with the theory of gravity. To a certain extent he realised the enormous age of the earth, and that fossils were the remains of creatures several million years old. Perhaps his most important scientific idea was that Nature was governed by certain forces, which when properly understood would enable man to use Nature for his purpose. Apart from his theoretical work, da Vinci was an important engineer, designing new towns and fortifications which would withstand cannon fire.

The Beginning of European Supremacy,
Heard and Tull.

Task B:

Read the passage above and make notes for an answer to this question: 'In what ways was Leonardo like a modern scientist and in what ways was he not like a modern scientist?

Now try the following procedure on other people:

(1)   select a fairly long piece of text;

(2)   tell people simply to 'read it and make notes';

(3)   then ask them a specific question about the text, like Task B;

(4)   now give them another text of similar length and difficulty to the first, but this time let them know in advance the question they will be asked;

(5)   ask the question, and note the differences in performance compared with the earlier test.

Everybody reads better with a task to focus the reading, and the younger and more inexperienced in reading the learner is, the more he or she needs to have their reading focused by precise tasks and questions. For our purposes, all our students can be thought of as 'inexperienced learners'. Our safest presumption, at least with students under age eighteen, is that it will never be appropriate to set a task quite as bald as 'Read Chapter 2', or even 'Read Chapter 2 and make notes'. So the main question we ask about a book, when deciding whether to choose it for a class, is 'Can I readily set specific tasks on it?'

There are some preliminary questions to ask first, though. The first is about the book's vocabulary, especially its use of abstractions. Books for schools very often fail to state the age-ability group for which they have been written. Even when they do say who the book is for, some authors have surprising ideas about suitable vocabulary in a book for, say, 'average students of 14'. So take nothing for granted.

When we come to assess the suitability of the vocabulary in a book, if we bear in mind our purpose of task-setting, we can do better than merely forming a general impression that a book is 'a bit hard' or 'about OK'. We can ask ourselves: 'How many translation tasks would I feel I had to set on a typical page before I could safely proceed to using the other skills?' Students do not have to be able to translate accurately every term on a page to be able to do useful work on that page, but in the 'Leonardo' passage we just looked at, they would certainly have to be able to translate 'scientists' and 'scientific' to make much sense of any other tasks.

All readers have some facility in slurring over words or phrases they do not fully grasp. You would probably say you fully grasped the whole of the 'Leonardo' passage. But can you really explain the phrase in paragraph one, 'would upset the balance between God and man . . .'? Even if you can't, though, it does not detract significantly from your grasp of the passage, and you probably did not even pause over it. The really important and hard question to answer is 'How often does this author use terms which I don't think my students know or are ready for and which are central to the understanding of what he is writing?'

The second preliminary question is about density. The following passage occupied 7¼ lines of print in a textbook. Count how many names, dates, facts it contains.

Charles IX died in 1574 and was succeeded by his brother Henry III (1574-89). When Henry's younger brother died in 1584, the Roman Catholics feared the throne would go to the Huguenot Henry of Navarre. To stop plots to depose him, Henry III had the Roman Catholic leader, the duke of Guise, murdered by a monk in 1589. Henry of Navarre then became King Henry IV and defeated the Roman Catholics.

It is fairly obvious that, although the vocabulary is not notably difficult, it is a hard passage to read, or to set useful tasks on. Usually, however, books are not like this all the way through. So it is usually possible to *avoid setting pupils to read passages dense with names, dates and information*. However, if such passages are very common or actually typical of the book, don't choose it.

The third point to look at is pictures. Good pictures can constitute a reason in themselves for choosing a book. By 'good' we mean, of course, as in the case of the text, 'forming a useful basis for a wide range of tasks'. We could say that a good picture has plenty of activity in it, usually involving people – but you might find that you could set many good tasks on a picture that broke both those rules. The safest course would be to pick a few of the pictures most typical of the book's picture-style, and see if it is possible to think up five or six questions on each one. If it is, that might be a good enough reason to choose the book.

It is possible that you 'pass' a book on the score of vocabulary, density and pictures, and yet when you try to work with it, find it difficult to devise good tasks. This might be because the author's approach or style, or something about the text, puts you off. The time to find this out is before you order fifty copies of the book, not after. In other words, the final test of a book's 'usability' must be whether you can actually use it as the basis for tasks.

Exercise 3

For practice, in assessing 'usability' see how many tasks, using all the cognitive skills if possible, you can make up about the 'Leonardo da Vinci' passage. Then try it on this next passage, which contrasts with it in subject-matter, style and tone, but is broadly similar in length and vocabulary level.

Japan made a treaty of alliance with Great Britain in 1905, and when war began in 1914 Japanese troops very quickly captured German fortresses and bases in China. Japan also made money by selling munitions to the Allies, and began to increase her factory production of cotton and other goods. As hours of work were usually very long, wage-rates very low and conditions in the workshops poor, the price of Japanese-made goods of all kinds was usually well below those which had to be charged by European nations, especially Great Britain, where work-people were much better treated.

Competition between Japan and other countries for world trade became very keen, with the Japanese leading and gradually obtaining a larger and larger share.

Pride in Japanese achievements and a desire to extend Japanese power led to the building of a large battle fleet and the upkeep of a large army. A 'war-party' of admirals and generals managed to obtain power. Those Japanese who believed in democracy were deprived of power or murdered. Manchuria was attacked and seized from China in 1931. Then followed other attacks, on Shanghai and Chinese coastal cities. At the same time huge quantities of cheap, mass-produced articles and cloths, 'made in Japan', were sold all over the world. The Emperor became the symbol of warlike Japan, which needed new lands for its hard-working, ambitious and constantly increasing population.

In 1937, an alliance between Japan and Germany was joined by Italy under her dictator, Mussolini. Hitler hated Communist Russia. So did the Japanese. In 1940 Japan, Germany and Italy signed a treaty promising aid to one another. The Japanese had long before this ended their friendship with Britain, partly because the Chinese received help and trade from the British through Hongkong and the Burma Road. The United States were also hostile to the Japanese, and stopped Japanese settlers from entering California or the Hawaiian islands. However, the Japanese signed a non-aggression pact with the U.S.S.R., in April 1941, and did not fight when Hitler invaded Russia two months later. They were still fighting against Chinese guerrillas in China itself, and they took over northern Indo-China and air bases in French Indo-China after the French collapsed in 1940, and refused to withdraw.

While meetings between the Japanese and Americans were being held to discuss these and other questions, Japanese aeroplanes and submarines were secretly brought close to American bases in Pearl Harbor and the Philippines; they prepared also to attack Hongkong, Malaya and the British. Without declaring war, the Japanese suddenly attacked Pearl Harbor on December 7th 1941, and quickly gained startling successes.

History for Today,
T.H. McGuffie, Macmillan, 1967.

Using Unsatisfactory Books

For all sorts of reasons, teachers have got stuck with books they would not have chosen, but have to use with a class none the less. Nothing can make such a situation satisfactory, but there are a few ways of making it less bad.

One way is to avoid use of the unsuitable books as much as possible by writing your own information sheets for students. This is a particularly suitable move if the problem with the book is that its vocabulary is too difficult. It is also a lot of work. If it is not to be an overwhelming task, you will need a very clear idea of what is the minimum information content necessary for the work you want to do. One way of approaching that question is set out below, taking, say, the case of the 'Leonardo' extract; supposing we wanted to write an information sheet as a substitute for this passage, because it was conceptually too hard for our needs.

Stage 1. Work out what the main concept is that you want to work on – in this case, not the concept 'scientist' (or we could use the text as it is), but some more concrete notion. One that would illustrate the case here would be the idea of a 'power source'.

Stage 2. Rough out the tasks we want to set, e.g. 'Say what you think a power source is', 'What sort of power source would a helicopter need?' 'What power-source would do for a paddle-steamer?' 'Which of Leonardo's inventions worked least well? What had they in common?'

Stage 3. Write an information sheet giving as much information as students need to do the tasks: in this case, not much more than a list of his innovatory activities in the field of mechanics might well be enough.

Using Very Small Sections of a Book

If the main problem with a book is that its text is already dense and full of information rather pithily expressed, then summarising it into information sheets is not going to be much use as a technique. So we can use another approach − using very small parts of the book at a time.

Look at how many tasks can be set on even a tiny, fairly dense passage like this one:

> After the German defeat and collapse in May 1945, the whole of
> Europe was occupied by the Allies. German leaders like Hitler
> and Goebbels had killed themselves in Berlin; Goering and many
> German military leaders were imprisoned; Himmler, leader of the
> Gestapo and S.S., committed suicide soon after British soldiers
> had hunted him out of his hiding place. The Russians occupied
> eastern Germany, and the British, French and United States
> armies had their 'Zones of Occupation' in the west. Berlin itself,
> the German capital, now in ruins, was inside the Russian zone,
> but all four main Allies took over a 'sector' in it; the city was still
> the home of hundreds of thousands of Germans.
>
> *History for Today*,
> T.H. McGuffie.

(1)   Say in your own words what a 'zone' and a 'sector' are.

(2)   Why do you think the Allies imprisoned some German military leaders?

(3)   Why did all the Allies have a 'sector' of Berlin?

(4)   Were the Allies right to imprison German military leaders?

(5)   What would the Allies have done with Himmler if he had not killed himself?

(6)   What might have happened if the Allies had not occupied Germany?

(7)   Could you describe the Allies as 'Imperialists'?

(8)   What's the difference between a 'leader' and a 'military leader'?

Exercise 4

Suppose that you thought the extract on Japan you worked on in

Exercise 3 was so dense that you wanted to give students only very small reading tasks — how many tasks can you make up on just the last paragraph of that extract?

Obviously, you would be in real trouble with a book if you were having to set readings of four or five lines! But learn to see a page or less as being a possible amount of reading to form a useful basis for work, if necessary.

Finally, remember the pictures as a source of tasks, even if all else fails and the text is really difficult and frustrating to use.

3. An Approach to History Field-Work

Suppose we took out a class of students in a bus to look at a well-preserved early nineteenth-century woollen mill, and some well-preserved workers' homes built at the same time, near the mill.

We must first be clear in our own minds why we would be doing such a thing. One good reason for a field visit is motivation. If the students had been led to work better at some in-school tasks by the promise of 'field-work' then that might be justification enough for the activity, provided that we did not spend much time on it. But there is a lot more that we can get out of it.

The mill and the houses can serve the same sort of function as the exhibits in a museum — they can act as strong concrete referents or hooks for strengthening concept-learning. The procedure for planning a visit to the mill, therefore, is in principle no different from planning for a museum visit, or indeed any other learning activity in the history/social studies field.

First, you work out what the concepts are that are necessary to an understanding of the site, and also what other concepts might be handily strengthened by a visit to the site. You have to visit the place in person, of course, to do this properly.

In the case of our mill, with younger students, we might well concentrate on two main ideas — the concept of a *site*, and the idea that the way buildings and places are is not accidental, but is determined by rational principles which students can figure out for themselves. This is not as simple as it sounds. The trouble with field-trips, as a learning experience, is that they are very confusing; the learner is bombarded with all sorts of quite irrelevant experiences — the journey, the packed lunch, the weather, losing his scarf, and so on. The problem is very well known to junior-school teachers who ask children to 'write about the trip to the beach' and get responses such as: 'We all waited but the bus was late. In the bus we had ice-cream soda, and tomato sandwiches, and we saw a horse in a field. Tony was sick and then we got to the sea and then came home.'

So getting across ideas about the rational siting of the mill, ideas which to us are pretty obvious, may not be too easy with excited younger students. But we are getting ahead of ourselves. The second main idea we will want to strengthen is the idea of *evidence*, and the understanding that buildings can constitute evidence for things, just like sources can.

We might add one more concept to this list of basic essentials — perhaps in this case the idea of 'cheap' as in 'cheap housing' — the sort of idea which field-work can make concrete in a dramatic way that no other kind of work can equal.

So we have the list: 'site', 'evidence', 'cheap'. Our next problem, of course, is to decide which tasks the students will do, using which cognitive skills. Some teachers, faced with planning a field-visit, fall back on approaches which they would not use in the classroom — a 'guided tour' type of lecture in which the learners are quite passive, or having the students complete a questionnaire about the site which deals only in factual information. So what could we do to do better?

A better way would be to use as our basic device an individual task-sheet for each student. It will contain tasks of interpretation, such as:

(1) 'Why do you think the mill is built where it is?' — broken down for less able students to: 'Why is the mill near the stream?' 'Why is it also quite near the bridge over the river?' 'Why is it not on the river itself?' and so on.

Application tasks such as:

(2) 'In what sorts of ways do you think they tried to keep the houses *cheap*?' — and made easier for less able students by giving clues like 'Why are the ceilings so low? Why are the windows of the houses smaller than those in the mill?'

Evaluation tasks like:

(3) 'We have been learning in class about documents being *evidence*. How useful are the mill and buildings as evidence for what life was like in those says?' — broken down to an easier version in perhaps this form: 'What can you tell from the houses about how

people lived? What can you not tell, but would need to read documents to know?'

The tasks need not all be of this kind — the students will probably be pleased at finding a slate on one of the houses that says '1811' on it, and want to tell you about it, so set a number of simple information finding tasks like 'When was the mill built?' as well as the tasks directly on the concepts.

The occasion is also a good one for using translation skills of the less usual kind, like sketching and making rough maps on the actual site, so 'Make me a sketch-map, trying to show me with as few words as you can why the mill is built where it is' would be a good style of task.

As with any kind of work, it will be vital to prepare students beforehand and make absolutely clear to them what they are supposed to do and why. The task-sheet, for example, should be given out and gone through, and if necessary explained, well ahead of the trip itself. And if field-work is going to be a regular, worthwhile part of your activities, it is arguably more important to follow up the visit with work obviously connected with the visit. It will be hard for students to take future visits seriously if you don't do that.

Progression in Field-Work

It is easy to get on to a sort of plateau of difficulty with field-work, and have students of sixteen, say, being asked very much the same sorts of question about a site as young students of thirteen.

We can try to guard against this in three ways. First, we can try to set tasks involving more difficult concepts. In the case of our mill and workers' houses, it might be possible to set application tasks like this in connection with the visit for older students: 'Look for evidence to support or attack the idea that the owner of the mill was paternalist in his attitude to workers.'

It will not always be possible to think of tasks in this order, because buildings as evidence are not always very eloquent on matters of that kind. Usually possible, though, would be our second move: increasing the number of factors students must take account of, by asking them to compare the mill site with other sites. We could ask, for example, an evaluation plus interpretation task like this: 'Are the workers' houses better or worse than contemporary ones in the town we saw last week? If you can see a difference, either way, try to think of reasons for it.'

The third thing we can do is, again, to make students deal with more factors by taking them to more complicated sites — a complex of buildings of different periods, built for different purposes, for instance.

Unless you live in an area unusually full of settlements, remains and buildings suitable for field-work, it is pretty obvious that your work in this area will have to be planned around those relatively few sites which are available, if field-work is going to be a major part of your approach. That gives rise to questions which only you can answer — building x may be available and easy to visit, but that does not make it worth visiting necessarily. Field-work is a 'high-prestige' activity, like discussion or games, and so we are tempted into treating it as an end, not a means, and accepting less cogent answers to the questions, 'What will students learn?' 'Is this the best way of learning it?' than we would in the case of more ordinary work.

On the other hand, field-work has high prestige partly because it deserves to have it. In terms of student motivation and involvement, and in terms of setting up good learning, it can be arguably more powerful than any method, if used well.

4. Planning Sequences of Lessons and Activities for Different Kinds of Classes

So far we have tried to deal with two main things — how to work out what concepts you want students to learn and use, and how to make up tasks in which they could use them. So far, though, mostly what we have actually worked out is single tasks or little strings of tasks. We now have to work out some principles on which to construct whole lessons and series of lessons, taking realistic note of things like available time, examination pressures, the different attitudes to work of a twelve-year-old and a seventeen-year-old and so on.

Case One

First we will consider a fairly easy case. A class of thirteen-year-olds of average to slightly higher than average abilities. No one in the class has special reading difficulties. There are no harsh pressures from examinations, so you have been given a fairly free hand in these terms: 'Try to get through the early days of the American Colonies, up to about 1700 in about ten sessions (each session is 40 minutes long) and cover Drake and Raleigh and the Armada, and all that, at the same time.'

There are some fiercer constraints though. You are told this about the class on reliable authority: 'These kids like to get all the facts, they like to get their note-books well filled. They don't like discussion or fancy stuff.'

Books and other materials are adequate — you can get a few relevant pictures, the main class textbook is a possible base for tasks.

You have written out a list of main concepts to be worked on, which looks like this: colony (colonist, colonise), explorer, pirate, economic, strategic (as in 'economic reasons . . . strategic reasons'), invade, treaty, alliance (ally).

Making the Scheme of Work for the Ten Sessions

What we have is a list of concepts, a set of constraints and a body of historical material. Exactly how we turn all that into a detailed scheme of work depends largely on our individual mental make-up and characteristic style of attack on problems. The following method offers some advantage though, and could be worth trying.

Ignore all constraints to start with — student expectation, time, historical chronology, everything and just write down your good ideas for student activities, as they occur to you. Note down which concepts these activities will be addressed to — (if you have to extend your concept list, do so). You may not use all the ideas, in the end you may not use any of them, but never mind. What you are doing is starting to impose a framework on the material, a framework which is based on your central concern of student learning.

Suppose, as a result of this 'brain-storming' process, you came up with ideas like these:

(1)   Comparing Spanish invasion of England attempt, 1588, with English 'invading' America — application tasks — is 'invade' right word? Evaluation tasks — morality of Spaniards and English colonists. Discussion work? Concepts — invade, colony, pirate (Drake).

(2)   Comparing Virginia and Massachussetts — 'strategic colony' and 'economic colony'. Work on Raleigh — idea of different motives. Classifying exercises, synthesis work. Concepts — strategic, economic, *motive* (new concept — not in original list).

(3)   Students choosing sites for colonies, off maps real and invented. Game — discussions on colony sites. Concepts — colony, economic.

Check out the concept list to see if there are any not being dealt with so far, or any new ones. In this case the concepts 'treaty', 'alliance', 'explorer', are missing, and 'motive' is a newcomer to the list. We must now decide what to do about the newcomers and the concepts *not* covered. In this case a reasonable decision would be to add 'motive' to our list of target concepts, decide to work in 'treaties' and 'alliances' with the Indians to the work on Virginia and Massachusetts and drop 'explorer', since the emphasis of our thinking seems to be swinging away from the exploration angle anyway, towards settlement.

We can now make a very rough plan, like this:

(1)   Virginia − site − selection, motives of settlers.
(2)   Massachusetts − compare and contrast with Virginia.
(3)   'Meanwhile, back in Europe' − 1588, Armada, etc.

Assume an equal distribution of time between the three elements, unless there is a strong reason not to. Now think about *lesson one*, in detail.

Lesson One

The first problem is how to begin. To start with the concept pre-test would not be a good idea. We have to work it in somewhere, but not at the start of our contact with a new class, unused to our ways.

Normally, we could suggest this rule for the very beginning of a lesson: always plan for three things: arousing interest, making clear what pupils are to do; involving all pupils in activity other than listening to teacher at an early stage, preferably within ten minutes.

These principles might yield a start like this:

(1)   Explain that class is going to hear a story, that the story contains a mystery, and that the class will be asked to try to solve the mystery (1 minute).

(2)   Tell story of disappearance of Roanoke colonists (5 minutes).

(3)   Class as individuals rough out answers to extrapolation task − 'What might have happened to the Roanoke colonists?' (10 minutes).

(4)   Answers evaluated by class in terms of plausibility of explanations given.

(5)   Pre-test.

There is an important constraint, though, which that procedure would ignore: the class are not used to this kind of work, and 'like to get their notebooks full'. So we must make a modification. Without dropping the three fundamental principles of a good start, we must give the class some, at least, of the kind of learning experience with which they are familiar — note-giving; setting of frameworks by the teacher; and rather more teacher-talk than we would ideally have. The revised Lesson One might therefore go like this:

(1)   Explain that for the next few weeks we are going to learn about early days in North America, and about Drake and Raleigh (2 minutes).
(2)   Give the class dictated note or cyclostyled note of main data, names, etc., of the topic (5-10 minutes).
(3)   Tell Roanoke story, set class to extrapolation task on 'what might have happened to colonists' (10 minutes).
(4)   Explain, and give, pre-test.

One vital element in both of these plans may have struck you as a pretty glib suggestion — the telling of the Roanoke story. It may be that there isn't a nice story like that conveniently to hand and that it is impractical to start *every* session with something 'interesting'.

We could helpfully extend the idea of 'tell a story' to the wider idea of 'putting an idea into a concrete setting and introducing actual people'. Then we can see that the technique is really of quite wide application, not very difficult, and not dependent on exciting stories that just happen to be lying about. Take a case — the origins of the American Civil War — not at first sight a particularly easy topic to start off interestingly. Here is how you might do it, by telling this little 'story'.

Suppose you were in an army, in a battle, and you suddenly realised that the people on the other side you were firing on were friends you used to go to school with, or maybe one of them was even your brother or even your own father; well that sort of thing really happened to people in America, in a great war that happened just over a hundred years ago. How could such things be? Well, we are going to imagine that in the year 1861, in Maryland, a man called John Starter, who was on one side, is having an argument with his brother-in-law, called Christopher Payne, who was on the other. Note down in your books, now, what they said, in a summary form, and I will note it up on the board. First John Starter said, 'Look, Christopher, I'm a Southerner like yourself, but I know that negro slavery is wrong, and has to go, and go without delay.' Christopher said, 'I don't like slavery too much as you know, but I think the question of if it goes and when it goes, and how it goes, is for those Southern states who have got slavery to decide for themselves.'

And so on. What comes out, in the end, is merely a pretty straightforward summary of the Union and Southern cases; but to put the case into the mouths of two real or imaginary protagonists is a simple, but very powerful, device for injecting interest, and making it 'a story'.

The traditional starting method, 'Recapping on last lesson' is a very difficult procedure to make interesting, and if it consists of putting questions to individuals about what they remember (or probably don't remember) of last time, it can easily destroy all interest at the outset. If you think it necessary to recall the previous session, do it either:

(1)   Very briefly – 'Last time we learned how the Civil War started – now today I'm going to tell you a story about . . .'

or

(2)   more fully, but *not* at the beginning – e.g.,

   (a) *story* about Wolfe at Quebec;

   (b) *work on* (e.g.) problems of conquering a distant, primitive country in the eighteenth century;

   (c) then, well into the lesson, when interest is well established, and pupils have had time to settle to the work and orient themselves, we could say – 'Last time we learned about Clive in India – who remembers what *his* problems were – how were they different?'

The basic idea is to plan for any recapitulation you want to do as carefully as for any other element in the lesson and not just 'stick it on the front' of the lesson.

Exercise 5

Write some 'story' type beginnings to new topics, or lessons within topics, on the lines of the American Civil War example above, then try devising some on topics where there is no clear debate to put into the mouths of protagonists, e.g. the industrial revolution, the Great Discoveries. How could these topics be 'personalised'?

Now to get back to our original lesson-series on the early days of the American Colonies.

Lesson Two

The problem has one new dimension now – you have the evidence of the pre-test. Let us suppose that one item 'economic' was particularly badly explained by students and to some students was not apparently even familiar as a word. The pattern of the lesson could be:

(1)　Express pleasure at 'results' of pre-test: do not mention poor result on 'economic'.

(2)　Say, 'Today we are going to do some interesting and slightly unusual work with maps.' Note that devices for securing interest can be very simple and economical – we have just used two in that sentence, namely:

(a)　claiming that what is about to happen will be interesting and novel;

(b)　promising work with maps, which, on the whole, students like – as they like stories, films, slides, 'quizzes', trips out of school.

(3)　Set tasks on colony site-selection (10-15 minutes).

Explaining a Concept – 'Economic'

(4)　Say, 'One thing a colony had to do was set itself up in such a place as to be safe from attack, as you figured out in the work we just did (stage 3). Another thing the colonists had to look out for was this: they wanted a place that would be good for trade, a place that would grow good crops, that they could sell some day, a place that would grow the kind of crops that people back home would buy, a place maybe with minerals they could dig up some day and use or sell, like iron or gold. When people think about getting rich, making money, selling crops and so on, we say they are thinking about the economic side of things. If we had chosen site B on the map for our colony, because it had gold mines, even though it was hard to defend, then we would say we had gone for the site for economic reasons' (5 minutes).

(5)　Set conventional, familiar reading and note-task on book – 'Make notes of pages 20-22, note down especially the economic reasons for the Virginia colony, and see if the book says the Massachusetts colony was likely to do well on the economic side of things' (15-20 minutes).

When you have to explain a concept from the ground up, as it were, remember three things:

(a)   If you can, try to set up some possibly relevant experience beforehand. In this case, students were working on site selection; not necessarily thinking in overtly economic terms, but probably in terms like 'good harbour, good place for a fort, trees useful for home-building'. The teacher can then refer back to that recent concrete experience, as when he says, '. . . if we had chosen site B on the map . . . then we could say . . .'

(b)   Build the picture of what the concept is all about, in as concrete terms as you can, before introducing the term. In this case the student met ideas like getting rich, money, gold, crop, iron, buy, sell before meeting the new word 'economic'. This way is, according to Piaget and others, more efficient than the more traditional fashion of explanation, 'Economic means . . .'

(c)   Follow the explanation with work for the whole class using the concept, as soon as possible – in this case there was an application task, and an interpretation task, both based on a book.

Exercise 6

If we were really in the position of having to explain all the concepts in your original list for this lesson series, from scratch, as it were, we would obviously have badly miscalculated the level of thinking of the class. But suppose for the sake of this exercise that you had to explain all the concepts in our original list, i.e. colony, pirate, economic, strategic, invade, treaty, alliance, motive. Plan out brief but detailed explanations in each case. (You can explain 'ally' instead of alliance, and so on, if you find it easier.)

Lesson Three

So far, our planning of lessons one and two has illustrated these principles: introduce new styles of work slowly, mixed with styles of work familiar to the student; try to plan the start of each lesson with particular care. Three big problems remain:

(1)   students' differing abilities;
(2)   whether to work in all the cognitive skills over three lessons, or ten lessons, or whatever;
(3)   whether or not to stick rigidly to the original scheme of work.

First, differing abilities. We can start taking appropriate notes of differing abilities as soon as we perceive them. By the end of lesson two of the series, for instance, we will have noticed that some individuals write less than others, and that they write less well. It is not probable that we would yet be able to be much more specific than that, let alone designate an 'abler' or 'less able' group in terms of conceptual level.

So we introduce at this stage the simplest of our devices, i.e. we let the less able write less, and yet still be successful. We might rough out an exercise like this: 'Here is an imaginary list of people, with the jobs they did, who wanted to go to the Virginia colony (actor, soldier, carpenter, silversmith, doctor, wagon-driver, shipbuilder . . .): write a little bit on each one, saying if you would let him go on the first colonising voyage, or not.' Thus we allow the less fluent to write quite small amounts, yet to show by the subtlety of their cases for and against whether their lack of fluency shows lesser understanding or not. The more able can write more on each item, and also get further down the list.

As to problem 2 — trying to get all the skills deployed in the course of about ten lessons would not be an unreasonable rule of thumb. Consciously to say to yourself — 'They have not had application (or synthesis or whatever) tasks for a while, I must try to think of one, if I can' — is a very reasonable way to approach planning. In the present case we might note that there has not been much application in sessions one and two, and that 'economic' has emerged as a concept of particular interest to us. We could quite deliberately try to think up some application tests on these lines — 'Suppose Raleigh planned to use Virginia as a base to attack Spanish treasure-ships, would that be an "economic" use of Virginia?'

Problem 3, how closely we should stick to our original plan, is more difficult. Suppose it emerged already, in lesson two, that students were somewhat thrown by our apparent disregard for chronology, and asked 'Why are we doing Virginia and Massachusetts all together? — Massachusetts is not until 1620, the book says, and Drake and everything and the Armada is before that.' Perhaps that would be a good enough reason to change the planned order to: Virginia; Drake, Raleigh, Armada, etc.; Massachusetts.

However, nobody wants to be a 'headless chicken' type of teacher, running around from one plan to another. Equally, nobody wants to be a robot. The point to hang on to is this — if you make the change which circumstances seem to be suggesting, you must still be able to see your way through your original plan, without having to abandon important concepts. On this test, doing Drake and the Armada second, not third, in the sequence looks all right. So we could properly make that change of plan if the students will feel more secure that way.

Exercise 7

Plan lessons three, four and five, of the 'colonies' sequence, *either* sticking to the original scheme of work *or* changing it to the order: Virginia; Armada; Massachusetts.

Case Two

Now let us consider a harder case — a group of fifteen-year-olds, of generally above average ability, working for an external examination.

The first thing we must do is get hold of some examples of the type of question they will be asked in the examination, so that we can work out an appropriate policy. Suppose these were typical examples on our 'set period': European History 1870-1960.

(1)   Describe the foreign policy of Bismarck between 1871 and 1890.
(2)   Give an account of the involvement of European powers in Africa, 1870-1900.
(3)   Why was the League of Nations unsuccessful?
(4)   Describe and explain the loss of imperial power by any *one* European nation after 1945.
(5)   Why did the USA become so involved in European affairs after 1945?

Clearly, these questions all set a major problem of analysis. Question 4 gives a little more help than the others, breaking the task into 'describe' and 'explain', but generally, the questions are very bald. They do, of course, all involve a formidable synthesis task, and also the understanding of a truly formidable range of concepts.

The first thing we must do, therefore, is pre-test not only the grasp of the class on some of the relevant concepts, but their level of skill in analysis and synthesis.

A test of analysis would look something like this — 'Last term you learned about x — look up your notes, and write down the points you would make in an answer to this question (set question in form typical of examination questions). Never mind about the order of the points, just put them down as you think of them.'

It might be too hard, if you start work in September, to have the class think back to work done in June, so you may not be able to test their analysis powers until you have covered some ground with them yourself. You can test synthesis, however, straight away. Give them a set of 'points' of your own devising on some question familiar to them and ask them to arrange them into an actual written answer.

It is important to separate skill in synthesis from skill in analysis, and to separate both from a conceptual grasp, so far as you possibly can, if you are to help students effectively. Just giving 'practice in answering questions' will not do much good by itself.

Consider this actual example of a student's work:

Explain the Rise to Power of Mussolini [first two paragraphs only]
Mussolini's party, Fascism, was both left wing and right wing.
On the left were the socialists and communists, and on the right
Republicans and Monarchists and big business. In between were
working class. The two sides conflicted with violence, from 1918
to 1922, as many ex-soldiers like Mussolini returned unemployed
from War. And Fascism answered their problems.

Mussolini's main ideas were some reforms, like the 'Battle of
Wheat', increasing Italy's population. But most of all he looked
for glory and battle in wars; Corfu, Abyssinia, Spain and then World
War Two.

In this piece so far we can see evidence of failure to synthesise well, and of failure to analyse properly what operations the question wants the student to perform, and also evidence of failure to grasp concepts. But all these evidences are mixed up together, so that the question 'Where would we *start* in helping this student?' becomes a very difficult one indeed — too difficult for a busy teacher with thirty such scripts to sort out very successfully. Such are the limitations of the 'Give practice in answering questions' approach.

Student Attitudes

As well as bearing in mind the urgent need to find out about their powers of synthesis and analysis there are the other constraints to make our task harder than it was in Case One. Notably, and obviously, there is the fact that students are not likely to respond well to work that does not seem to be directly relevant to success in the examination. Their idea of 'relevant' might well be very narrow. On the other hand, we might expect a good response if we make clear exactly how the work we do might help them to pass, and this gives us an extra motivational weapon we did not have in Case One.

Making a Scheme of Work

Suppose we were planning twelve sessions on the period 1870-1914, as a start. We know we can expect students to be asked questions on diplomacy – probably Bismarck, 'Eastern Question', origins of World War I. Another area fairly sure to 'come up' is European imperialism; possible but not certain are areas like working-class movements, or some question of economic history.

We work out our concept list in this fashion: 'foreign policy', diplomacy, alliance, entente, Power (as in 'Great Power'), economic, imperialism, political (politics), tariff, free trade, socialism,liberalism.

We can make the same first move as we did in Case One, that is, ignore all the constraints and write down good ideas for student activities as they occur to us, then check the ideas against the concept-list to see if we need to add to the list. (We are, of course, now not so free to take concepts out of the list at this point, as we did with 'explorer' in Case One.) Finally, we make a rough plan, maybe like this:

(1)   How people made up 'foreign policies'.
(2)   Bismarck's foreign policy as an example.
(3)   How the Industrial Revolution went on after 1870.
(4)   Imperialism.

Lesson One

We might get away with starting with a concept pre-test, in this case, introduced by some formula like – 'Now we are going to approach this question of doing well at the exam in a really organised fashion. Half the secret of success is having a really good grip on the meaning of a couple of dozen words; also, enjoying our work and getting a lot out of it for our own sakes has a lot to do with how well we understand some of this sort of language – so I want to see first just where we all stand on these words . . .'

After the pre-test, we can start up a system of cycles of work, extending over a period of two or three lessons, which we stick to for a long time, maybe the whole year. Here is a possible example:

Phase One. Take a key term – 'foreign policy', explain it, set application tasks in general terms using it (e.g. 'Which of these items would fall under "foreign policy"?'), also translation tasks – 'Give examples of items of foreign policy from work you have done before' and other tasks in general terms, for example, evaluation, 'What would a good foreign policy try to do?'

Phase 2. Conventional style work based on books or teacher-provided notes, using the key term, e.g. 'Which of this list of things Bismarck did were "foreign policy"?' 'Was his foreign policy successful?' We can use our original 'good ideas' of the early planning stage, in Phase 1 and Phase 2.

Phase 3. Set medium-scale synthesis tasks using the idea, like comparisons of German and English foreign policy in short essay form.

You can vary the details of the cycle, of course, for instance sometimes taking pairs of contrasted ideas as your start-point, like 'political', 'economic' or little groups of related ideas. If you make sure that the timing of the cycles remains tight, you will secure three good results. First, the students learning ought to be much better if they are meeting ideas in an orderly fashion, explained in simple terms, before they meet them head-on in their reading. Second, making application of the concepts to the material of the course in Phase 2 an inflexible part of your plan, and making synthesis tasks or 'little essays' also an inflexible part of the plan, you will be helped to keep to the syllabus and less tempted to get into large-scale activities, say large-scale simulations, giving undue weight to one or two concepts. This will, in turn, tend to create, students' confidence in you and your procedure. You want them to feel, ideally, that work with you is interesting and unusual, but also purposeful and directed closely to their goal of the examination. Nobody has to be dull because they have an examination-oriented class. What you have to be, to be fair to such a class, is purposeful, and as keen to 'cover' the syllabus in your way as they are in theirs.

Exercise 8

Take a topic of your choice. Work out what you think are two or three of the main concepts on which the topic hinges. Write brief explanations of each one, and then devise as many short tasks as you can, of as many different types as you can, to illuminate that concept and deepen students' understanding of it. Plan so that the whole thing, including initial explanation, will only take half an hour.

Revision for Examinations

We can make good use of our classifying and reordering of materials exercises at the revision stage (see section on classification). Also at this stage, if not before, students must have practice in analysing what is required by the standard question forms of the examination in question, such as 'How far was . . .', 'Explain . . .' and so on.

Case Three – A Senior Class

For this case we will postulate a class of seventeen-year-olds, of above average to very high ability. They are probably working towards some advanced level examination, though in a more leisurely way and with more teaching time per week available, than in Case Two. One of the traps we might fall into with such a class is to assume, because of their age and ability, that they do not need to practice the analysis of examination questions and the synthesising of answers. This is very unlikely to be true of all such students.

The analysis they will have to do on questions is more difficult than the class in Case Two had to do, in four main ways.

(1)   They may have to make more complex analyses, as in a question like 'How have historians' judgements of the peace settlement of 1815 changed over the years?' Here they have to work out what kind of thing to say about the 1815 settlement, and also what kind of thing to say about what historians (which ones?) say about it.

(2)   The clues about what kind of response to give get more cryptic, they go from 'describe' and 'explain' at the lower level of examination to, for example, a quotation followed by the gnomic instruction 'Discuss'!

(3)   Very high-level abstractions, such as 'significance', 'critical analysis' are likely to occur in the questions they meet in the examination.

(4)   The synthesis tasks are likewise large – Hitler and Stalin, domestic affairs and foreign, and so on, commonly having to be dealt with in one question.

It is very probable that the class will profit from small-scale exercises in analysis and synthesis, in just the same way as the class in Case Two. In fact, to cut the matter short, no important element in the teaching approaches we have discussed becomes superfluous just because the class is seventeen years old and bright. Setting a good concept pre-test will be just as important, making a motivating and interesting start to sessions just as important. The problem is that this group differs from the others in the matter of student expectation.

Student Expectation

The class in Case Two probably had developed their own theory of examination-passing and of teaching, expressed in some formula like 'What you need is a lot of facts; a good teacher is one who gives you a lot of facts.'

The class of Case Three will probably have a more refined set of theories, some helpful to you, others not. Their theories might go like this: 'What you really need for the exam is facts. We should be allowed to express opinions, too – so there should be discussions. A good teacher is a good talker – lively, tells jokes, makes things interesting, while getting through the facts. Some of the time, at least, history is no longer just a school subject to us – the issues are real and emotionally charged; we care about some questions and see contemporary relevance in them. Acceptable work for us to do is – listening to lecturing, having discussions, writing essays. Unacceptable "kid's stuff" is things like tests, small-scale writing exercises, anything with pictures or maps, being asked the meaning of words.'

If the class have a set of opinions like this, it is helpful to the teacher in these ways – you might expect favourable response to discussion work; to games and simulations where the discussion-element is stressed; to the consideration of abstract ideas; to work involving evaluation.

Not so favourably received might be direct translation or interpretation work. If you ask a student right out 'What do you think "Fascism" means?', he might be more embarrassed and defensive about being unable to give a clear reply than a younger student would be. Also he might be more emotionally involved in working out his attitude to Fascism than in trying to define it closely. He may be ambivalent about many highly charged political terms – he wants to use them in argument; he wants to win arguments using them; he could resent attempts to make him define them, and see such attempts as challenges.

Similarly, with books – he will be using adult history books by now, and his use of them is important to him as a sign of maturity. An interpretation exercise that shows that he does not understand large chunks of the books he reads could meet a lot of resentment.

Even in activities of which the class might approve, you could hit snags, particularly in discussion. You will want to set up discussion with learning goals in mind, stressing application of concepts, extrapolation and the like. They will probably see discussion as most people see it – as an occasion for winning arguments. They will want their discussion to resemble adult 'outside world' discussions, and derive satisfaction from taking part in rambling, diffuse, emotional exchanges such as they see on television, even though you don't think much of them as learning occasions.

To sum up – they will have by now their own ideas about what ought to be happening in history classes, ideas connected with their perception of their own dignity and status as near-adults. These perceptions are not illegitimate – just not always helpful. What to do?

To get over this problem, it might help to think in terms of a cycle of activities, as in Case Two. One way to plan a cycle might be like this. We could work it out backwards. Session 4 could be the 'target session' as it were, in which the class will discuss at length some question such as 'Were Metternich's policies justified or not?' Also round about session 4 they will be embarking on a major piece of written work with a title similar to the question put to focus the discussion. In sessions 1 to 3, we prepare for this grand debate. As individuals or groups, the class work basically on analysis and synthesis tasks on a small scale, working out arguments and counter-arguments on aspects of the debate. They also work on translation and application tasks, involving the major abstractions which will come up, e.g. liberal, represssion, censorship, nationalist, conservative, middle class. We present these tasks not as bald challenges to the student, but in forms such as – 'The other side, the anti-Metternichs, are going to accuse Metternich of being "repressive". Let's figure out a good definition of that word, then read about what he did in Austria and see if we can't show that it didn't amount to much repression. If we can't show that, maybe we can look at the 1848 revolutionaries, and see if we can make out that they were as "repressive" as Metternich.'

We can use all our 'good ideas' in this phase, trying to work in extrapolation work, evaluation work, or whatever. When the great debate arrives in session 4, the debate should be of higher quality because of the preparatory work, but we need not worry too much about that, we will have managed to get what we want – intensive work on small-scale tasks – in sessions 1 to 3.

Setting up a debate as the 'target' is just one method, the principles are the important thing which we might review in this way:

(1)   The students need to do small-scale tasks with clear goals, just like any other students.

(2)   We need to take serious account of the hostility they might feel to doing such tasks 'like kids'.

(3)   We need to set up as it were dignified short-term 'targets', like a debate, to establish a need for the small-scale tasks.

(4)   The whole little cycle of tasks and 'target' must produce conventional visible outcomes, like essays and notes, which are plainly useful in terms of the examination to come.

(5)   As in Case Two, we should make the cycles short, so that we are seen to be covering the syllabus at a reasonable speed.

Exercise 9

Plan a cycle of work for seventeen- to eighteen-year-olds on the lines just described *either* with a 'debate' or some other activity as the 'target' for the final session.

4 'ATTITUDES' AND EVALUATING PROGRESS

1. 'Attitudes'

Our emphasis throughout this book has been heavily on people learning skills, concepts, information. Teachers are also interested, rightly, in other aspects of students' learning, less measurable, more pervasive things, which are sometimes summed up under the general heading of 'attitudes'.

All teachers would agree that they should try to foster favourable attitudes to work, to school, to doing their particular subject. We could usefully pull together here the main recommendations we have made so far about this, as we worked on the different skills. We might note:

(1)   The importance of genuine acceptance of students' opinions and judgements, particularly in discussion, in evaluation work and extrapolation work.

(2)   The importance of making sure students understand the teacher's plans and proceedings and the precise purpose of their work. This is a universal rule, but particularly important when introducing new styles of work.

(3)   The importance of students having success, and being praised for it – especially less able students.

(4)   The importance of good feedback. Students must see their written work being treated with respect, and being used as a useful basis for future progress.

(5)   The importance of making some move to interest and motivate students, in every session, however simple and unelaborate that move might be.

If a teacher is seen by students to be at least trying to observe these five principles, the chances of gaining co-operation, approval for himself and his subject, and generally 'good attitudes' will probably be greatly improved.

There is a second group of attitudes, which is more specific, but yet sufficiently general for all teachers to approve of them in principle. Under this heading we would have mainly the scholarly values, ideas like 'respect for truth', 'respect for evidence', 'willingness to suspend judgement until all evidence has been considered', and so on.

Some people consider that the study of history in itself is likely to promote these attitudes. On the face of it, this seems pretty unlikely. History can quite well be taught as a series of authoritative judgements (known to the teacher) based on well-established facts (known to the teacher). Even if a great deal of apparently free discussion takes place between students and teacher, it is quite easy for a teacher to 'win' all the time, by mere fluency, or by introducing evidence not known to the students at the outset of the discussion, or simply by the weight of his authority. This is an unlikely way to produce 'respect for evidence', but quite a common approach, still, to teaching history.

If we really want people to have those particular attitudes, we must make clear to them that these attitudes are admired by us, and reward them, with praise and, where appropriate, with good grades, when they are manifested. Hardest of all, we actually have to display them ourselves. This is really quite difficult to do, when you are surrounded by people (students) who have less knowledge of the relevant evidence than you do, and who are vastly less skilled in interpreting and evaluating and presenting it. Merely being presented with the results of scholarship cannot make anybody scholarly.

A further discouraging circumstance is that students do not notice this particular set of attitudes being exemplified or apparently greatly valued in the world outside the classroom. Even professional academics do not always feel it necessary to back up assertions with evidence when they are talking about, say, contemporary politics, or education. So, by all means, try to foster these attitudes; in fact it would be difficult in conscience not to try — but have no illusions about the size of the task.

The third set of attitudes is the contentious set, e.g. 'attitudes' like 'a favourable attitude to the underdog', 'tolerance for people of other countries and creeds', 'hatred of war and oppression', 'appreciation of the value of their own country's role in the world'.

Around this point we can get very near setting up as a goal that students come to share our opinions, under the guise of 'forming good attitudes'. Whether it is right to do that is a moral and a private matter. It might be worth noting though, that researchers are pretty discouraging on the possibility of teachers affecting student attitudes in controversial areas, and particularly pessimistic about teachers actually changing pre-existing attitudes.

Broadly, the picture seems to be this. Other influences, such as the home and the peer-group, are much more powerful than teachers in attitude formation. Teachers are quite likely to produce an effect the exact reverse of what they are seeking. This seems to become more true, the more overtly and vehemently the teacher puts his own view.

So, if you want to make them hate the Fantasians, the best policy seems to be to tell them enthusiastically what a great people the Fantasians are! (Alternatively, you could choose students whose parents are confirmed Fantasia-phobes.)

Two Things to Read on 'Attitudes'

1. H.C. Triandis, *Attitudes and Attitude Change*, John Wiley, 1971.
2. L.M. Watson, 'Cigarette Smoking in Children', *Edinburgh Health Bulletin*, no. 24 (of more general application than the title suggests).

2. Evaluating Students' Progress

It is important that we know whether or not we are succeeding as history teachers. Leaving aside for the moment the question of students passing or failing examinations, we can succeed or fail at two levels, the level of general aims, or of specific objectives.

'General aims' cover long-term goals like 'to make students better citizens', 'to give them a historical perspective', 'to make them historians', 'to get them to understand themselves better as people'. Figuring out whether or not a general aim has been achieved or partly achieved by, say, the end of a year is usually difficult, sometimes just about impossible.

In the case of the aim 'to make them historians', we could write a list of characteristic ways in which historians usually behave, like the kind of things they say when faced with a statement or question about the past, or with a piece of documentary evidence. We could then give students examples of such statements, or lists of evidence at the start of a year, and at the end of the year, and see if the kinds of things they said about them had altered.

With the other examples of general aims quoted, it would be harder to make up such a test, and in the case of 'To get them to understand themselves as people', one feels a bit unclear about what such a test might even look like.

Perhaps the importance of general aims has been over-written. Teachers don't seem to go about testing whether they have achieved them and people often react unfavourably to the idea of testing at all in this context. Very similar syllabi and methods are used by teachers whose avowed general aims are very different; teachers don't really seem to spend much time thinking about general aims at all. What your own general aims as a history teacher are is your business – but one interesting exercise to try would be this: what sort of test could you imagine that could check out whether or not your general aim was being achieved, with a given class, after one year?

Then there are specific objectives, which fall into three broad classes: concepts, skills, information. The first two are obvious enough – no general aim of any kind could be achieved if students were not significantly increasing their grasp of concepts, and their expertise in the cognitive skills. The third, whether or not students are learning information, is the easiest thing to find out and also easy to get confused about. Suppose we have been teaching about the post-1950 independence movements in Africa. Let us consider exactly what information we would want students to be able to give us, in say a straight recall test, a week or so after we finished the work.

We could usefully divide the information into two parts. First, illustrative information – they must clearly be able to give some examples to illustrate concepts like 'nationalist leader', 'new nation', 'ex-British territory', 'ex-French territory', 're-named territory', 'colonial war', 'federal state'. Two examples of each, perhaps, might be reasonable to ask for.

'Uhuru' means 'freedom'. 'Accra is the capital of Ghana.' 'The Algerian war started in 1954.' These are examples of information not illustrative of any particularly abstruse concept but which inevitably come up in talking and reading about the topic of post-1950 Africa. Is any one of those three items more important than the other two? Would you care if students could not remember any of them? Would you care if they could not remember them in a year's time? These are questions to which you can only give your own answer, but one thing is obvious – we should be quite clear in our own minds exactly what we want the students to learn in this area of 'secondary' information, i.e information not illustrative of a particular important concept.

Thus, when we write our initial plans, the section on 'information objectives' should look something like the following. 'Students should be able to recall: (a) two examples of nationalist leader, new nation (and so on); (b) dates of Ghana independence, Algerian war, capitals of Ghana, Nigeria, approximate population of Africa in 1960' – or whatever you think necessary.

No use at all is to plan like this: 'information objectives – general information on Africa, climate, etc.; main outline of independence movements'. Such planning would actually imply that students have to learn maybe 100,000 items of information ('general information on Africa') which is a lot for three or four sessions.

It is hard discipline, to ask ourselves exactly what pieces of information we really want people to recall, because it makes us face the unpleasant fact of the massive scale of student forgetting. We have to do it, though, if we are to evaluate sensibly the success of our teaching from the angle of information-learning. Above all, we must get clear the difference between mere information and information needed to illustrate and thereby strengthen the grasp of a concept.

The problem with concepts and skills is the reverse of the problem with information. There is no problem specifying what concepts we want 'learned', because they have been on our mind right from the stage of planning the outline scheme of work. In planning individual sessions, the section 'Specific Objectives – Concepts' is easy to fill in.

As for skills, we are also pretty clear about which ones we have in mind to emphasise in most sessions. But how do we evaluate students' advance in understanding of a concept, or improved expertise in a skill? Let us look at concepts first.

Suppose we had pre-tested someone's understanding of the term 'mercenary soldier' in two ways.

(1) a straight translation question: 'What is a mercenary?'
(2) an application question: 'Were German soldiers in World War I mercenaries?'

At the pre-test, we got these responses from the student:

(1) Mercenaries are cruel soldiers.
(2) Some might have been not all.

Now suppose we do work on Renaissance Italy, some of it directed to improving understanding of the idea of a 'mercenary soldier'. We then give exactly the same two questions to the student as a 'post-test' and get these responses:

(1) A paid soldier.
(2) No. They had to fight (conscripts) in World War I.

Now the understanding shown is still not perfect (for example, the model response to question (1) might be, 'volunteer, paid soldier, willing to change sides quite readily for better pay, loyal to commanders, not to states or nations'). However, these later answers certainly represent a visible advance towards the ideal answer. If we had time and inclination we could probably divide the 'understanding' of the term 'mercenary' into nine or ten stages and say that the student had advanced from stage two to stage five, or something of the sort, but as teachers we must settle for a positive answer to this question: 'Has the student's understanding of the concept advanced at all?' In this case we can say that it has. Usually, though, real life is not as clear-cut as that. For example, these following responses to the same two questions:

(1) *What is a mercenary?*
    (a)   A soldier who will do anything he is told.
    (b)   Soldiers especially good at fighting.
    (c)   Soldiers who don't mind what side wins the war.
(2) *Were World War I German soldiers mercenaries?*
    (a)   Yes, they had to obey orders.
    (b)   Yes, they were good fighters.
    (c)   No, they wanted Germany to win – would never fight for someone else, or France especially.

In both cases, the answers under (c) have now got the idea of the mercenaries' lack of moral involvement in the wars of the time, and we could say, mark a clear advance, although they don't make the point on payment which is central to our ideal answer. The sets of answers (b) and (a) say things about mercenaries which might sometimes be true of mercenaries or of any soldiers. They present, however, an advance on the possible confusion with the word 'merciless' which may well be the origin of the initial pre-test answer, but it looks like a very slight advance.

In these real-life responses, we can note two things: (a) we need a pretty clear understanding of the concept ourselves to detect whether an advance has taken place; (b) an answer can show a real advance, but with an emphasis that is not what we had in mind, as student (c) emphasises moral detachment rather than money.

Exercise 1

Work through these examples now. In each case a pair of pre-test responses is given, and three 'post-test' responses. What you have to do is work out which of the post-test responses represents an advance in understanding and, if you can, which represents the greatest advance, which the least. Assume that the 'post-test' responses are paired, i.e. in the post-test 1 (a) and 2 (a) are from the same student, and so on.

Example 1 (twelve-year-olds)

Unemployment

Pre-test questions

(1)   What is 'unemployment'?
(2)   Can you give an example of an unemployed person?

Response (pre-test)

(1)   When people don't work.
(2)   Old people.

Post-test responses (same questions)

(1)   (a)   If people cannot go to work.
      (b)   No work to do for the people.
      (c)   People idle all day at home.
(2)   (a)   Sick or aged people or children.
      (b)   Depression between the wars.
      (c)   If your factory closed.

Example 2 (fourteen-year-olds)

Depression (economic)

Pre-test questions

(1)   What does the word a 'depression' mean?
(2)   Suppose a lot fewer children were born, and so a lot of teachers lost their jobs — would that be a depression?

Responses (pre-test)

(1)   People losing their jobs for a long time.
(2)   Yes.

Post-test responses (same questions)

(1)   (a)   Mass unemployment world wide.
      (b)   Trade got less so people would lose their jobs.
      (c)   People have less money, so spend less on things, so less money all round and so on.
(2)   (a)   No, unless happening all over world.
      (b)   No, must be to do with money.

(c)   No but yes, maybe you could say 'a depression for teachers'.

Example 3 (seventeen-year-olds)

Rationalism (context of eighteenth-century Enlightenment)

Pre-test questions

(1)   What is a rationalist?
(2)   What would be the attitude of a rationalist to the Christian Church?

Responses (pre-test)

(1)   Open minded. A person who listens to all opinions.
(2)   He would be tolerant, allow people to choose which sect or religion they wished to belong to.

Post-test responses (same questions)

(1)   (a)   Liberal-minded, in the context of the eighteenth-century Enlightenment.
         (b)   In favour of a scientific approach.
         (c)   Weighs up reasons before deciding for or against a particular view.
(2)   (a)   He would have opposed its cruelties in the eighteenth century.
         (b)   Thinks Christianity is false.
         (c)   Agnostic, but would value all opinions.

Example 4 (fourteen-year-olds, very able)

Absolute King (seventeenth-century context)

Pre-test questions

(1)   What does it mean to say a King is 'absolute'?
(2)   Is the Queen of England today 'absolute'?

Responses (pre-test)

(1)   The only King in a country.
(2)   Yes, but Duke of Edinburgh helps her to rule.

Post-test responses (same questions)

(1)   (a)   A King is absolute when no-one else has sovereignty.
         (b)   He has right alone to make and declare laws.

(c) He is the only one with soldiers in the country.
(2) (a) No, because Parliament has sovereignty in England now.
(b) No, Parliament and Commons make some laws.
(c) There are police and army does not all belong to Queen (except Guards) (so No!!).

For this exercise, we presumed that the way you would test the success of concept-learning would be by a test using the same type of question, or even the same actual question, as you used on the pre-test. That is the most straightforward way to do it, and probably gives the most accurate picture. But you don't want to do this all the time. You don't want to give students the impression that you are 'test-crazy'; also, you will not always want to wait until the end of a teaching cycle to check out the students' progress.

So a lot of the time, you will be trying to evaluate students' progress on the basis of longer pieces of speech or writing than a short test-answer. Let us look at a few examples.

Exercise 2

In this exercise, try to evaluate in the case of the responses to the tasks whether the students are demonstrating an advance in understanding of the concept in question, compared with the understanding of the concept in question shown by their pre-test responses.

Student A:

Concept – Conquer (1066 context)
  Pre-test: 'What does it mean if somebody conquers a country?'
  Pre-test response: If one side wins the battle, that is conquering.
  Later application task: 'After they conquered England, the Normans want to conquer Wales. Make up a plan how they might do that.'
  Response: 'Fight a battle and win in Wales somewhere maybe the North. Kill some of the Wales people to scare others. Build castles, get Saxons to build them, so if Wales army attacked you would be safe.

Student B:

Concept – reactionary (nineteenth-century Europe context)
  Pre-test: 'What is a "reactionary"?'
  Pre-test response: Violent ideas. Person with ideas very strongly held.

Later application task: 'Write a short piece as by a reactionary
person, about the idea of Prussia having a written constitution.'
Response: The idea is a disaster. Total collapse will break out,
Prussia will no longer exist as a nation. All freedom will be lost.
The Country might be destroyed in a few more days by France
or Russia.

Student C:

Concept — economic imperialism (nineteenth-century China context)
    Pre-test: 'How is economic imperialism different from any other
sort of imperialism?'
    Pre-test response: If a country puts its colonies to economic use,
not just e.g. as naval bases.
    Later application and interpretation task (discussion): Focus your
discussion on this: Suppose someone said: 'The West were not
Imperialists in China — they seized hardly any territory except
Hongkong, and China was independent the whole time.' Draft a
reply as a group, agreeing or disagreeing, with reasons.
    Response: [evaluate only student C's contributions]
        Student C: Well, Hong Kong was used for trade and . . .
        Student X: I think he means the rest . . .
        Student Y: The rest of China. The main bit.
        Student X: They sold them, sold them railways and machinery,
ships. They sold them at a big profit and made them pay . . .
        Student C: That's just selling, that doesn't make it Imperialists.
        Student Z: Economic Imperialists.
        Student C: Only if they forced them. If they sailed up and said,
'You've got to buy all this cotton or anything or we will take over
the country and be a colony or blow up Pekin.'
        Student Y: They did go in 1900 Boxer . . .
        Student Z: They could force them in other ways. Could say
make them buy or we won't let you sell your stuff . . .

Student D:

Concept — capital (as 'capital city')
    Pre-test: 'Say in your own words what the capital of a country is.'
    Pre-test response: Main town. The one where most people go, and
most live.
    Later extrapolation task: 'Suppose Borovia City the capital of
Fantasia was destroyed in an earthquake, what problems would
that make for Fantasia?'

Response: Buildings destroyed. Dead people. Disease. Many casualties. Nobody knows what to do. President or King would have to go round and make orders, but might be dead himself, so new King needed. Elections for new President or King. Elections would have to be at Borovia City, but not possible now.

Student E:

Three concepts together in this example: political, economic, social
 Pre-test 1: 'What would you say politics was to do with?'
 Pre-test 1 response: Elections, how people vote for. Choosing Presidents.
 Pre-test 2: 'What does "economic" mean?'
 Pre-test 2 response: To do with money.
 Pre-test 3: 'What would "social history" be about?'
 Pre-test 3 response: Less important things.
 Later evaluation and synthesis task: 'What do you think were the most important results of the Civil War? [America, 1861-5] Remember that we have learned about political effects, and also social and economic effects.'
 Response: I think most important was in politics. U.S.A. kept together, and had same President in both parts and so were strong enough for World War I and to win Cuban war in 1898. This was important. The U-boats might have beaten the U.S.A., if the U.S. had been split up.

 Economic effects is next. Gold was found in California in 1849, there were railroads built to California. Population grew, and industry grew up everywhere. Black people now get paid instead of being slaves so people began to accept black people, slowly, because they had their own money and economies now. Some worked in factories. The Cattle Kingdom might not have happened to be so great in 1885 if Texas had been in one country and Chicago in another in the North. Cattle would have had to cross a border now and there could have been outlaws on the border.

 Dress changed a lot after the war, especially for women, but that was not the war I think. Other big social changes were changes in outlook with the meteoric rise of the robber barons. People changed in many social things.

Evaluating Progress in Skills

The special problems of evaluating progress in skills are fairly obvious. First, if you introduce a new skill to students, say extrapolation, you can probably get a visible surge of improvement in competence, from their first fumbling effort, to about their third or fourth attempt, by which time they have begun to form an idea of what is involved. After that point, though, progress is likely to be slow and therefore hard to detect. Second, in the case of some skills, like translation, it is difficult to separate the idea of progress in the skill from progress in understanding the ideas which are being translated (except in the case of exercises with maps and pictures and graphs, of course).

On the first point, what we can do is look for progress in skills over a longish period, say half a year. As to the second point, we can say this: in the case of some skills, we can say pretty clearly whether a person is getting better or not, in fact we can virtually quantify it: evaluation work and extrapolation work depend largely for their quality on the number of factors of which a student can successfully take account.

Equally, in the case of analysis, we can say that if student A is doing better than student B in, say, analysing what is required in a project, what he is doing is working out *more* of the sub-tasks that need to be done than B is.

With synthesis it is difficult to describe why one student's synthesis is better than another one, but, happily, pretty easy to recognise when it is so, which is good enough for our present purpose of evaluating progress. (Of course, it would not do to tell a student that his synthesis of essays and so on was not good enough, in certain incommunicable but vital ways. For purposes of giving students feedback, we have to get down and say exactly what is wrong.)

That leaves translation, interpretation and application. Except in the case of work with graphs, maps and so on, it is probably not of practical use to try to separate progress in the skill from progress in understanding the material involved in using the skill, in the case of translation and interpretation.

The case of application is a little different. Look at these two examples of response to an application task:

Task: A country has an elected President, everyone can vote in the elections for president. This country is also divided into counties. The counties are ruled by councils, but people do not vote for the councils, they just have the ten richest men in the country. Is the country a republic?

Response A

All the people vote for President which is right, but there are no county votes which is not fair, people should vote in county as well.

Response B

No, because people in the counties don't vote, only rich men.

Both responses show the same lack of understanding of the concept 'republic'. But B is a better piece of application — it says clearly whether the concept will apply or not, with reasons.

Students can fail to carry out application tasks properly in more sophisticated ways than the one quoted above, as in this case:

Task: When the allies defeated Napoleon and put Louis XVIII back in France, was that a *revolution?'*

Response: They really had no choice, Napoleon could not be trusted after the 100 days. They could not have a republic, as Austria would not have allowed that, or Russia indeed, therefore only the King of the House of Bourbon was left.

If Napoleon had stayed on would have been the true revolution if he had carried out to full measure the Spirit of 1789.

Obviously, this is not an answer to the question, not a piece of application at all, except for the veiled hint about 'true revolution'. So we might note the rather banal but important point that 'doing less well' at application might involve the student not doing application at all, but taking trouble to disguise the fact.

With application tasks, also, we can of course use the idea of 'number of factors used' as a measure of progress. Thus, as an answer to the 'France 1815' task we just looked at, Response A (below) would be better than B.

Response A

Yes, because (a) violent change, by force, of rule, (b) big change in the government, (c) changes in everyday life for peasants, etc., (d) peace would reign — a big change. Only a small revolution though; because changes would not be major like before 1789.

Response B

It could not be one because it was people from outside the country did it. The people did not rise up to affect changes.

As to which of these students has the better understanding of the concept of revolution — that is a different question.

Remarks on Exercise 1 (p. 182)

Unemployment

Response 1 (c) does not seem to show an advance, but the response 2 (c) has the important idea of unemployment not being voluntary. This shows the usefulness of having a two-barrelled test, and the way in which a straight 'Does *x* mean?' question can sometimes not be adequate in revealing understanding.

Similarly 2 (a) clearly shows up lack of understanding where response 1 (a) from the same student sounds pretty good.

Depression

Response 1 (a) illustrates an important point. Sophisticated language — 'Mass unemployment world wide' can sometimes mask lack of understanding quite effectively. Response 2 (a) seems to show that this student has, in fact, only latched on to the idea that depressions have to be widespread to count as depressions. Responses 1 (c) and 2 (c) are clumsily expressed, but have more of the idea, e.g. the idea in 1 (c) of a *cycle* of economic problems.

Rationalism

Response 1 (a) again shows how in a 'post-test' a student might merely clothe exactly the same level of understanding he had at the pre-test in elegant new language. Responses 1 (b) and 2 (b) seem to show clearest advance.

Absolute King

Response 1 (a) also shows up this same point, only now, with the addition of the term 'sovereignty', it gets confusing, because we don't know for sure what the student means by it. He might take it to mean 'power' in which case there has been a real advance, or he might mean something like 'the legal right to be King', in which case he is simply dressing up the original pre-test level of understanding. Response 2 (a), though, might well indicate that he takes 'sovereignty' to mean power.

Remarks on Exercise 2

Student A – Conquer

Certainly an advance beyond the idea of 'winning battles'. Still some areas of ambiguity revealed by the apparent continued existence of a 'Wales army', but basically a reasonable advance.

Student B – Reactionary

This is a tough one. A reactionary might indeed have said all these things, but the student seems to be emphasising the violence of the opinions as much as their content. This is a good example of the sort of response that we must accept as a 'good answer', and yet feel disquiet about.

Student C – Economic Imperialism

The most promising sign is when student C says the Westerners might threaten to 'blow up Pekin' – that is the only sign he gives of moving away from the idea that economic imperialism necessarily involves holding territory.

Student D – Capital

Much rather confusing mention of kings, presidents and elections indicates, probably, a grasp of the idea of a capital as a political centre, in his second response. The idea that elections have to take place at the capital is a nice illustration of a student putting his own, very concrete, interpretation on the idea of 'a political centre'.

Student E – Political, Economic, Social

Both 'politics' and 'economic' seem to have developed well beyond the original limited notions of the pre-test. 'Social' is obviously still pretty problematic to the student, and the probable lifting from a book of the phrase 'changes in outlook . . . robber barons' is a classic illustration of one of the standard moves made by students when they know they don't understand something: 'When in doubt, put something down that sounds good, straight out of the book if possible.' We should not be hard on students for doing this, it is only the equivalent of our adult trick of talking rather faster and using jargon when we don't really understand what we are saying. If you detected this tactic, though, it is a very reliable indicator of lack of understanding in the student.

Final Exercises

(1)   You can evaluate how much sense this book has made to you personally in quite a simple way. Look back at the five quotations from teachers at the beginning of the Introduction. What advice, if any, could you give those teachers now?

(2)   This book has been largely concerned with day-to-day problems of planning, carrying out and evaluating teaching tasks, so more general questions like the justifying of the place of history in the curriculum, or discussion of the ideal content of a five- or six-year history syllabus have not been directly addressed. However, it might be interesting to look at those two questions as a final 'exercise', as it were.

(a)   Justifying the place of history in the curriculum

Some of the justifications put forward for the teaching of history suffer from one or more of the following defects:

(i)   They are not justifications at all, but merely descriptions, as when we say 'History is the study of change in time', without saying why 'change in time' is worthy of study.

(ii)   They make claims which ought to be supported by evidence, and are not so supported — as when we claim that study of history helps people to form a sense of their own identity or makes them generally wiser, better or more agreeable than people who do not learn history, without adducing evidence to show that this is so.

(iii)   They make claims that history as a subject does certain things for people, without specifying that the history would have to be taught in a certain way to do these things — for example, in the 'attitudes' section we noted the implausibility of the common claim that history fosters independent thinking, in the context of some traditional history-teaching methods.

Can you justify the place of history in the curriculum, avoiding these three pitfalls?

(b)   The content of an ideal history course, for students of 11 to 18

Could you devise and justify such a course, in the light of a concern for development of a big range of specific concepts, and of a range of cognitive skills? How useful as guides are the linked ideas of concept development and skills in tackling this question?

ANNOTATED BIBLIOGRAPHY

A. Books

One could usefully make a start on reading up the general background of theoretical and innovative thinking with this small list of titles.

Barnes, D. and Britton, J. *Language, the Learner and the School*, Penguin, 1969

Bloom, B.S. *et al. Taxonomy of Educational Objectives, the classification of educational goals. Handbook 1 – Cognitive Domain*, Longmans, 1965

Bruner, J.S. *The Process of Education*, Harvard, 1960

Bruner, J.S. *Toward a Theory of Instruction*, Belknap-Harvard, 1966

Coltham, J. *The Development of Thinking and the Learning of History*, Historical Association pamphlet, no. 34, 1971

Coltham, J.S. and Fines, J. *Educational Objectives for the Study of History*, Historical Association pamphlet, no. 35, 1971

Fenton, E. *Teaching the New Social Studies in Secondary Schools*, Holt, 1966

Furth, H.G. *Piaget for Teachers*, Prentice-Hall, 1970

Hallam, R.N. 'Piaget and Thinking in History' in Martin Ballard (ed.), *New Movements in the Study of Teaching of History*, Temple Smith, 1970

Further reading could be based in the first instance on:

Fines, J. *A select bibliography of the teaching of History in the United Kingdom*, Historical Association, 1969 (Helps for students of History, no. 77)

Chaffer J. and Taylor, L. *History and the History Teacher,* Unwin Educational, 1975 (very useful summary)

B. Kits

It would also be very useful to examine a selection of the large number of innovative 'kits' and 'packs' of teaching material published in the last few years. Specifically on history, there are:

(1)   ILEA World History Project. W. Hewitt and J. Lockyear

(eds.). Heinemann

(2)   Place, Time and Society 8-13. Collins, for the Schools Council (individual elements include 'Life in the 1930s', 'Clues, Clues, Clues – work in History' and 'Shops')

(3)   Jackdaws. Jonathan Cape

(4)   Archive Teaching Units. Published by University of Newcastle-on-Tyne Education Department

(5)   Prehistoric Britain. I. and F. Morley. Edward Arnold

(6)   History Workshop. K. Brown. Macmillan

(7)   Longman's Grays Ltd. Resources Unit publish several History Games, e.g. 'Norman Conquest', 'Frontier', 'Canals'. Longmans also publish History Units, Secondary History Packs, History Project Packs

Many sets of material are published which are of great potential interest to history teachers, although described as 'General Studies', 'Integrated Studies' and the like. We might note especially:

(8)   The Schools Council/Nuffield Humanities Project. L. Stenhouse (ed.). Heinemann.

This scheme is massive and impressive.

The 'Teachers Handbook' is indispensable for anyone wanting to use discussion as a teaching method, and the sections in this book dealing with discussion have drawn heavily on its ideas.

(9)   Schools Council General Studies Project. Longmans and Penguin Educational (units include Africa, Living in Britain, Economics, The Development Puzzle)

(10)   Longmans General Studies Project (units include Man in Nature, Welsh Nationalism, The Sino-Soviet Dispute, Japan's Economic Miracle, World Population Policy)

(11)   The Childwall Project – Design for Living. Edward Arnold

(12)   Schools Council Integrated Studies Project. Oxford University Press (unit or sub-unit titles include 'Sense of History', 'A Complex Society, Imperial China', 'Children and the War, 1939-41')

(13)   The Taba Social Studies Curriculum – Hilda Taba. Addison Wesley

Also of interest are materials published in the form of records or audio-tapes, for example:

(14) The Sussex Tapes. Available from Devonshire Works, Barley Mow Passage, London W4

(15) Long-play records of the 'History Reflected' Series. Apollo Society/Decca Records

See also, the great range of BBC publications in printed, tape or record form.

GENERAL INDEX

aims, general 16, 179

Bloom, B.S. 12, 17, 18
books, use of 90, 111-20, 151-8
Bruner, J.S. 11, 12, 13, 17, 51

concepts: 'characteristic' 12;
definition of 14-15, explaining
26-9, 166-7; importance of, in
history-teaching 15-16; 'over-
arching' 23; partial understanding
of 28-9, 'pyramids' of 26, 33;
relationship of to intellectual
skills 34; selection of 23-6

discussion 65-71, 175; small group
71-3, 84-5

essay-writing 126-32; marking essay
work 133-8
examination classes 169-76;
questions 57; *see also* revision
exposition 164-5

'feedback' to students 133-8
fieldwork 158-61

games 62, 82-7, 89-98
generalising 139-42
graphs 38-9, 88, 132

information, historical 15, 180-1
information sheets 156

justifying teaching of history 192
judgements, moral 97-101, 104

language of tasks 56-7, 169, 173
level of difficulty of tasks 55-60,
74-5, 79-81, 88-9, 102-4, 122-3,
124-6, 129-30, 132, 143-51,
160-1, 167-8
library skills 124

maps 40-1, 132
mixed ability groups *see* level of
difficulty of tasks
motivation 121, 132, 161, 177

museums 47-8, 106-7

note-making 111-20, 122-3, 152-3

objectives 180-1

Piaget, J. 11, 17
pictures, use of 42-7, 76, 93, 107-10,
158
planning of lessons 161-76; of
syllabus 21-6, 192
pre-tests: for understanding concepts
29-33; of skill of analysis 118-19;
project work 120-6

questioning, oral 62-3

recapitulation 165
revision 63-4, 75-6, 173

sources, work involving 49-55, 64-5,
119-20
spelling 133
simulations 85-6
stories 163-5
spiral curriculum 12, 22-6
syllabi *see* planning of syllabi
structures of subjects 12
students: 18; attitudes of 170-1,
177-9; expectation of 174-5;
opinions of 51, 70-1, 93; powers
of expression of 35-6, 132-3

tentativeness, of historical knowledge
51, 107

'weasel' words 20, 23, 102

INDEX OF MAIN HISTORICAL EXAMPLES, IN CHRONOLOGICAL ORDER

DATE DUE